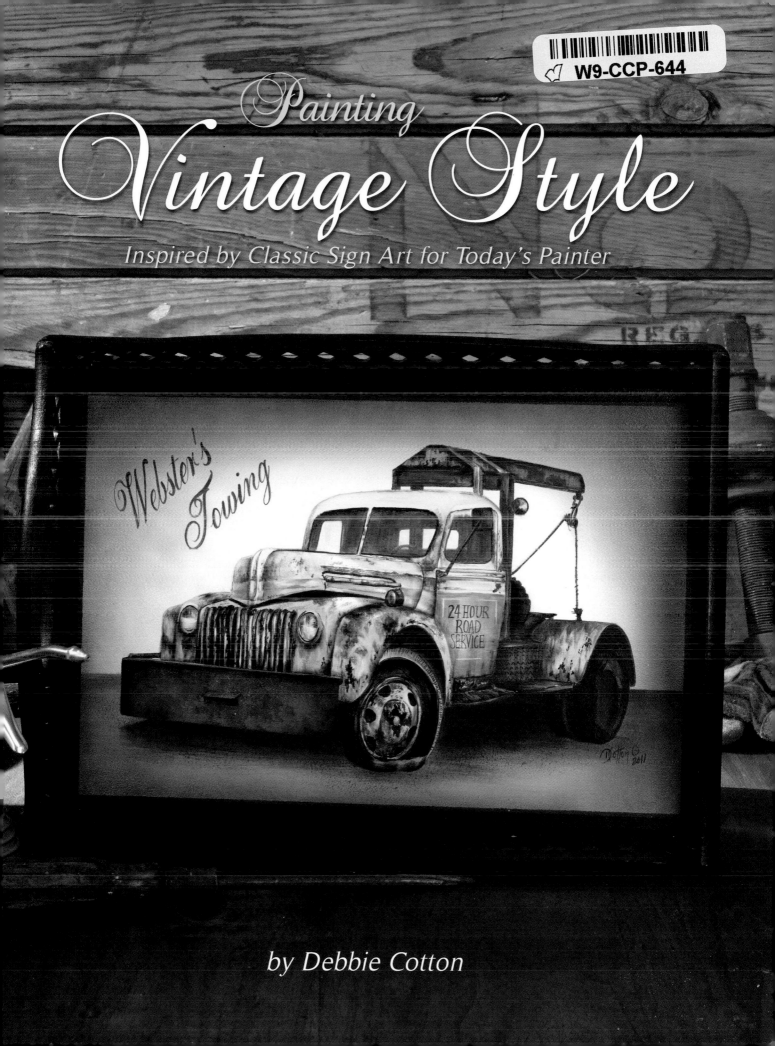

Painting
Vintage Style

Inspired by Classic Sign Art for Today's Painter

by Debbie Cotton

Published by

All American Crafts, Inc.
7 Waterloo Road
Stanhope, NJ 07874
www.allamericancrafts.com

Publisher | **Jerry Cohen**

Chief Executive Officer | **Darren Cohen**

Product Development
Director | **Brett Cohen**

Editor | **Linda Heller**

Proofreader | **Natalie Rhinesmith**

Art Director | **Kelly Albertson**

Product Development
Manager | **Pamela Mostek**

Printed in China
ISBN: 978-1-936708-10-9
UPC: 793573035332
Library of Congress Control
Number: 2011911044

www.allamericancrafts.com

Special Thanks to

Brett Cohen, Linda Heller, and the crew at All American Crafts for believing in me. They have been publishing my designs since 2004, and I am thrilled that they are now publishing my first book. I look forward to the journey ahead.

DecoArt, Princeton Artist Brush Co., and all the wonderful suppliers that have supported me throughout my career.

The team of Princeton Select Artists: Willow Wolfe, Holly Hanley, Lydia Steeves, Donna Scully, and Shelley Lanthier. On numerous occasions, they advised and encouraged me to publish a book. Well, ladies, I finally did it!

To my students and fans: Thank you for supporting the decorative painting industry and for enabling me to do what I love best—paint!

From the Author

We have all heard the saying, "Take a stroll down memory lane." Those words themselves remind me of a simpler time and bring back wonderful recollections of my youth. Memories of after-school chores and home-cooked meals, and times shared with family members and cherished pets, unite with visions of wild lavender and fresh blueberries growing amidst the foliage outdoors. As a young girl, I admired and held a certain fascination for things that were old. Century homes, antiques, and vintage cars inspire my creativity, and my designs reflect the uniqueness they possess. It is my wish that the charm and whimsy of the catchy slogans on my designs in this book help to create a vintage story that will take you back to more carefree days. I hope my painted signs not only help to restore and return life to some of the classics, but also inspire you to paint from your heart.

Dedication

I would like to dedicate this book to my family—they are my inspiration for everything I do and every choice I make. My husband, Todd, has been my rock for over twenty years, and has always helped me turn my dreams into reality. From completing the restoration of a run-down farmhouse that we now proudly call home to helping me create the catchy slogans for my vintage signs, Todd has always been involved in my painting palette. My two sons, Mitchell and Brett, have also been exceptionally supportive and encouraging. It still melts my heart when I recall one of the first art shows that Mitch attended: He wanted to help run the booth while I was busy teaching classes. At the end of the show, Mitch looked at me, smiled, and said, "Mom, I am so proud of you!" At the next show, it was Brett's turn to assist, and he was just as wonderful. He helped with everything, from taking care of sales in the booth to staying late and helping me pack up everything for our long journey home. I am so proud of the three men in my life, and I love them more than words can say. There may never be a dull moment, but I can't imagine it any other way!

Contents

NEW YORK KENNEL CLUB

Breeding
Champions
Since 1898

30

36

RKIN'S FRUIT WHOLESALERS

Freshness Guarantee

Hand Packed Since 190**40**

ALLEY CAT
LICORICE CO.
World's Finest
Ten For A Penny

44

48

WindyRidge
FARM

52

Basic Supplies

This section lists the supplies you will need to complete the projects featured in this book.

Brushes

◆ *Princeton Artist Brush Co.*
Select Series
 – ⅛" angular shader (Series 3750AS)
 – 1½" bristle bright (Series 3750BB)
 – Nos. 4, 6, 8, 10, and 12 chisel blender (Series 3750CB)
 – ⅛", ¼", ⅜", and ⅝" deerfoot (Series 3750DF)
 – Nos. 2, 4, 6, 8, and 10 filbert (Series 3750FB)
 – No. 2 Fix-It (Series 3750FI-2)
 – ⅛" and ¼" filbert grainer (Series 3750FR)
 – Nos. 8 and 10 flat shader (Series 3750FS)
 – ½" and ¾" flat wash (Series 3750FW)
 – No. 10/0 liner (Series 3750L)
 – ⅛", ¼", ⅜", and 1" lunar blender (Series 3750LB)
 – ½" lunar mop (Series 3750LM)
 – Nos. 0, 1, and 3 round (Series 3750R)
 – Nos. 10/0 and 1 script liner (Series 3750SC)
 – Nos. 18/0 and 10/0 short liner (Series 3750SL)

Synthetic Sable Series
 – 1½" flat wash (Series 4050FW)

Umbria Series
 – No. 12 flat (Series 6250F)

Other Supplies

◆ *Creative Imaginations* Impress-On rub-ons: Antique Accents (No. 28406) and Sepia (No. 28405)
◆ *DecoArt* Americana Acrylic Sealer/Finisher, Matte (spray)
◆ *DecoArt* Americana Multi-Purpose Sealer
◆ *Winsor & Newton* Winton Oil Colour: Raw Umber (for antiquing)
◆ Odorless thinner (for antiquing)

General Supplies

◆ Brush basin
◆ Clear plastic ruler
◆ Fine-grit sandpaper
◆ Kneaded eraser
◆ Lint-free rags (for antiquing)
◆ Painter's tape
◆ Palette paper
◆ Paper towels

◆ Pencil
◆ Soft cloth or tack cloth
◆ Sponge roller (for basecoating)
◆ Stylus
◆ Tracing paper
◆ Transfer paper (gray and white)
◆ Vinegar
◆ Water

Source of Supplies

All of the designs featured in this book adapt easily to a variety of surfaces. The following suppliers provided the surfaces and materials used for the projects.

COYOTE WOODWORKS
RR 32 52 Lee Valley Rd.
Massey, Ontario P0P 1P0
Phone: 705-865-1414
Fax: 705-865-2193
www.coyotewoodworks.ca
orders@coyotewoodworks.ca

DECOART
PO Box 386
Stanford, KY 40484
Phone: 606-365-3193 or 800-367-3047
www.decoart.com

JB WOOD PRODUCTS
1285 County St.
Attleboro, MA 02703
Phone: 508-226-3217
www.jbwood.com

PRINCETON ARTIST BRUSH CO.
PO Box 5256
Princeton, NJ 08543-5256
Phone: 609-683-1122
www.princetonbrush.com

SIMPLY COTTON
3851 Regional Rd. #57
Nestleton, Ontario L0B 1L0
Phone: 905-986-4463
www.simply-cotton.com
simplycotton@xplornet.com
Note: Simply Cotton is also the supplier for the Creative Imaginations Impress-On rub-ons.

VIKING WOODCRAFTS
1317 8th St SE
Waseca, MN 56093
Phone: 800-328-0116
Fax: 507-835-3895
www.vikingwoodcrafts.com

To become a member of the Society of Decorative Painters, visit: **www.decorativepainters.org.**

To become a member of Decorative Artists in Canada, visit: **www.daic.ca.**

Paints

DecoArt Americana Acrylic Paints were used for the projects in this book. I use many of the same colors in my designs; I find they work well together in the different stages of building values.

DecoArt Americana Acrylic Paint

Antique Gold Deep

Antique Maroon

Antique Rose

Antique White

Avocado Dip

Bahama Blue

Berry Red

Black Green

Black Plum

Bluegrass Green

Burnt Orange

Burnt Sienna

Butter

Cadmium Orange

Cadmium Yellow

Camel

Charcoal Grey

Citron Green

Cocoa

Colonial Green

Dark Chocolate

Deep Burgundy

Desert Turquoise

Dioxazine Purple

Driftwood

Evergreen

Flesh Tone

Golden Straw

Gooseberry Pink

Hauser Dark Green

Hauser Light Green

Hauser Medium Green

Heritage Brick

Honey Brown

Jack-O'-Lantern Orange

Khaki Tan

Lamp Black

Lemon Yellow

Light Avocado

Light Buttermilk

Light Cinnamon

Marigold

Milk Chocolate

Moon Yellow

Napa Red

Navy Blue

Neutral Grey

Payne's Grey

Plantation Pine

Primary Red

Primary Yellow

Sea Breeze

Shading Flesh

Slate Grey

Snow White

Soft Black

Tangerine

Terra Cotta

Traditional Burnt Sienna

True Blue

True Red

Tuscan Red

Ultra Blue Deep

White Wash

Yellow Ochre

DecoArt Americana Neons Acrylic Paint

Fiery Red

Brushes

Good-quality brushes are essential tools for successful painting results. It is important the brushes keep a good edge in order to properly execute the painting techniques used to create these designs.

Brush Care

Proper brush care is critical and will extend the life of your brushes. Acrylic paint dries quickly, so it is important to gently clean your brushes with water between colors. Do not immerse the brushes into paint up to the ferrule, because paint is very difficult to remove from this area when it is wet (and even more difficult when it is dry). Never leave a brush soaking in water for an extended period of time. When you are finished painting, use a good-quality brush cleaner to remove any paint residue. Reshape the brushes and lay flat to dry.

Princeton Artist Brush Co.
SELECT SERIES

Angular Shader

The angular shader is a flat brush with its bristles cut at an angle. This versatile brush can be used for sideload floating techniques and to paint sharp, defined edges. It can also be used on the chisel edge to paint a variety of flowers.

Bristle Bright

This natural bristle brush is 1½" wide and can be used to dampen a painting surface with water before applying sideload floating techniques.

Chisel Blender

This brush is similar to a flat brush with its squared-off bristles and sharp chisel edge, but the bristles are shorter, making it much easier to control and to float and chisel color onto a painting surface. This works well for creating wood grain and flower petals. The fine vein lines in a flower are created by chiseling from the center outward.

Deerfoot

The deerfoot is a short, natural bristle brush with its bristles cut on a slight angle. It is a great brush for stippling, and can be used to stipple background texture, greenery, and flowers. It is also used to stipple highlights and texture on fruit. Because its bristles are shaped on a slight angle, it is used on the flat for large stipples and on the tip for small, tight areas.

Filbert

The filbert brush has oval-shaped bristles that work great for basecoating individual design elements, allowing for smooth edges. I also gently fan this brush out to create C-stroke feathers for animals such as roosters, hens, and a variety of birds. The resulting stroke is rounded at the end rather than straight.

Filbert Grainer

The filbert grainer has oval-shaped bristles of uneven lengths, making it possible to create multiple lines with a single stroke. It is used to paint animal fur, grass, and long hairs. It can be used on the flat for fine lines or on the chisel edge for thicker, heavier lines.

Fix-It

This unique brush, which was designed by me, is new to the industry. Its hard bristles and slightly rounded shape enable you to easily remove excess paint or wet paint mistakes from your surface. Simply wet the brush, lightly scrub on the area from which you wish to remove paint, then pat the area with a paper towel. It may be necessary to repeat the process several times, but it works like magic! I suggest that you keep this brush handy for all of those "fix-it" jobs.

Flat Shader

The flat shader has longer bristles than a chisel blender, enabling it to hold more color. It is generally used for sideload floating and is available in a variety of sizes. When painting, choose the size that best fits the area you are painting.

Flat Wash

The flat wash is similar to a flat shader, but comes in larger sizes. It has longer and wider bristles, which work nicely when applying sideload floating techniques to large areas

Liner Brushes

Liner brushes are small, pointed round brushes with long, narrow hairs. For this book, I used short liners, a liner, and a script liner. It is important to choose the appropriate-size liner brush for the area you are painting.

The **Short Liner** has the shortest hairs and is great for small, fine details and smaller-sized lettering. Another use for the short liner is what I term skimming the surface, which creates an extra-fine highlight.

A **Liner** has medium-length hairs, holds more paint than a short liner, and covers a larger area when pulling linework. For the projects in this book, a No. 10/0 liner was used for the larger lettering, outlining, and medium-sized lines.

A **Script Liner** has the longest hairs and holds even more paint. It is used to create long, flowing lines.

Lunar Blender

This is very unique stiff-bristled brush that is used for drybrushing. Instead of scrubbing in a circular motion, drag the brush across the painting surface using either the flat or chisel edge, depending on the effect you wish to achieve. On the flat edge, it can be used to distress backgrounds and drybrush highlights. On the chisel edge, it can be used to create evergreens and foliage.

Lunar Mop

This thick, rounded brush has soft, natural, fluffy hairs and is used dry with a light pouncing motion to soften floated color, stippled color, and washes. Gently pat in an up-and-down motion to soften and blend the paint. As the brush picks up water and paint, gently drag across a paper towel to remove the paint from the brush.

Round

The round brush has full, round bristles that reach a tip at the end. The tip of the brush can be used for fine work, and the brush can be gently flattened when painting larger areas. It can be used to basecoat small areas and to create elements like flower petals wet on wet by gently blending the colors.

Princeton Artist Brush Co.
SYNTHETIC SABLE SERIES

Flat Wash

This large 1½"-wide synthetic sable bristle brush holds a large amount of water and paint. It can be used to apply a background wash and for initial sideload floating to create a wide shade or highlight.

Princeton Artist Brush Co.
UMBRIA SERIES

Flat

This Series 6250 brush has a beautiful Velvetouch finish on the handle, which is extremely comfortable to hold and use. Its long, premium bristles allow for a smooth gradation of color to clear water when used for sideload floating techniques. For the projects featured in this book, I used a No. 12 flat, which is 1" wide.

Tips & Techniques

Note: Follow all manufacturers' label instructions for proper product usage. Use caution when working with any flammable materials and dispose of cloths, etc. properly.

Antiquing

Antiquing is a finishing technique that is used to age a painted design. For my projects, I use odorless thinner (odorless thinner for oils, not methyl hydrate) and Winsor & Newton Winton Oil Colour in Raw Umber, but you can use whichever brand you prefer.

I like to antique around the outside edge of my painting surface, but not over the actual design, as I do not want to alter the colors of the painting itself. First, use a lint-free rag to rub the odorless thinner over the entire design; apply a liberal coat, not too heavy or too thin. Use the same rag to pick up Raw Umber oil paint and apply it around the outside edge of the painting, rubbing softly in a circular motion to fade. Continue to work the color in toward the design to soften. A mop brush can be used to soften the edges, but clean the brush frequently by wiping on a towel to remove excess moisture. If the Raw Umber oil comes in too far on the design, it can be easily pushed back. Working from the middle of the design out, gently rub a clean rag in a circular motion to remove the excess color. Continue to mop to soften edges. When finished, lightly mist the surface with matte Acrylic Sealer/Finisher to help set and dry the oil. Allow to dry thoroughly.

Basecoating

The term *basecoating* refers to the application of a solid layer of paint on the painting surface before individual design elements are painted. Several applications of the basecoat color may be needed in order to achieve adequate coverage. Allow each coat to dry thoroughly before applying the next one.

Basecoating can also refer to painting the initial coat of individual design elements. For a solid background, use the 1½" bristle bright or a sponge roller to ensure a smooth finish. When basecoating individual items, use a flat brush for elements with straight lines and edges and a filbert for rounded items (fruits, vegetables, and flowers). When painting a loose basecoat, use a chisel blender to randomly chisel through color; the resulting basecoat will have light and dark areas.

Drybrushing

This is a technique for using a dry brush with little paint to apply highlights and shading. Load the dry brush with paint, lightly drag on a paper towel to remove excess paint, then apply lightly to the painting surface by lifting and dragging the brush. The result should be a light brushing of color.

Floating

This technique is used to apply shading or highlighting, which adds dimension to the painting. Dip the brush into water, blot on a paper towel to remove excess moisture, then sideload by dipping a corner of the bristles into paint. Stroke the brush on palette paper, pulling it toward you, then lift the brush and continue to stroke in the same spot on the palette paper until you have a smooth transition of color across the brush. The brush should have strong color on one side fading to no color (clear water) on the other side. Turn the brush over, move to a clean area on the palette paper, and stroke the other side. Paint should now flow evenly through the bristles. Move to the painting surface, lay the brush flat on the area to be sideloaded with the darkest color against the edge to be shaded or highlighted. Pull the brush toward you as you apply the color. Let dry before applying another color.

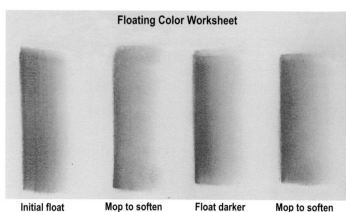

Floating Color Worksheet

Initial float | Mop to soften edges | Float darker value, but cover a narrower area | Mop to soften edges

Hair/Fur Technique

When painting hair and fur, take your time to build layers of color. Thin the paint with water to an inky consistency. Load a filbert grainer with thinned paint, gently fan the bristles into a fork-like shape on the palette (this will help you to achieve long, flowing hair), then apply strokes to the painting surface by lifting and pulling the brush toward you. Use a filbert grainer on the chisel edge for thicker individual hairs. You can also use a chisel blender; using this brush on the chisel edge will allow you to paint thick hair with long or short strokes. Use a liner for fine hairs and highlights. Make sure your strokes follow the shape of the area that you are painting.

Hair/Fur Technique Color Worksheet

Filbert grainer using flat edge | Filbert grainer using chisel edge

Lettering

Successful lettering starts with the basics. When you are tracing the pattern, use a ruler to create straight lines. I use a plastic ruler that bends, which makes it much easier when working on a round surface such as tin. I also use a large gridded ruler; the grid assists me in applying the letter pattern to a painting surface. Align the top and bottom of the letters with the top edge of your surface to ensure that the letters are straight. When tracing and transferring patterns for lettering, I find it easiest to first pull the horizontal lines across the top, middle, and bottom edges, followed by the vertical lines. The same is true when applying the paint. Use a suitable liner brush for the size of the lettering that you are painting. Thin the paint with water to an inky consistency. Turn your painting surface so that you are always pulling the brush toward you. Begin by painting the horizontal lines, then turn the surface and continue to paint the vertical lines.

Linework

Thin paint with water to an inky consistency. Load the brush and then apply to your painting surface, pulling the brush toward you for smooth, straight lines.

Skimming the Surface

When skimming on color, thin the paint with water to an inky consistency. Load a short liner with thinned paint, then lightly drag across a paper towel to remove excess paint. Move to the surface and pull the brush toward you, skimming the surface to create long and short lines. This is similar to drybrushing.

Stippling

This technique consists of using a dry brush with a minimal amount of paint to add shadows, highlights, and texture to a design.

Load a deerfoot brush with paint, lightly pounce on the palette to remove excess, then hold the brush vertically and softly pounce up and down to deposit paint on the surface. Mop to soften, if needed.

Stippling Color Worksheet

Stipple   Dampen surface, stipple, and mop to soften   Stippling wet on wet

Tints

Tints are light washes or floats of color added to an area to provide interest and intensity. They are generally applied in mid-value areas and help to balance a design. When applying tints to a design, the edges should be soft—you should never see a line. Mop to soften the edges, if needed. Tints can also be applied using a drybrush technique.

Using a Chisel Blender

Load a chisel blender as you would for a sideload float, but when applying to the painting surface, float and then pull lines out on the chisel edge. When chiseling, always lead with the clean (paint-free) edge of the brush. Depending on what you are painting, you may want to simply chisel the paint without floating; this works well for animal fur. Simply load the brush in the same manner as for a sideload float, but only work it once or twice on your palette. Hold the brush vertically upright near the end of the handle, lead with the clean edge of the brush and, using the chisel edge, pull toward you. *Note:* Holding the brush higher on the handle allows for long and short flowing strokes.

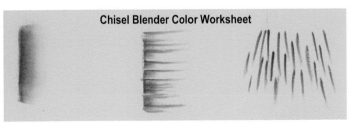

Chisel Blender Color Worksheet

Floating   Floating and chiseling   Chiseling

Using a Mop Brush

Lightly pounce a mop brush on floated color to soften and blend the paint, working from the water line inward. A mop brush is used dry; when you pat the floated color, it will pick up the moisture and paint. Lightly drag the brush across a dampened paper towel to remove the paint, then lightly drag on a dry paper towel to remove the water. Continue to mop.

Wash

A wash is a mixture of paint and water that is generally 80% water to 20% paint. Blend this mixture on your palette, load the brush, then lightly blot on a paper towel to remove the excess water before applying to the painting surface.

Wet on Wet

This technique refers to the blending of one color into another while the colors are still wet. Painting wet on wet is a fun and easy technique that helps you achieve instant results in your painting.

Sometimes it works well to stipple wet on wet. For instance, when painting the center of a flower with a deerfoot brush, begin by stippling a liberal coat of the medium value. Wipe the brush on a paper towel, pick up a small amount of the dark value, and stipple to blend. If the brush has too much paint in the bristles, wipe on a paper towel to remove the excess, then continue to stipple. While the paint is still wet, clean the brush in water, dry, pick up the light value, and stipple the highlights. Again, once you start to stipple the highlight value, you may have to clean the brush on a paper towel to remove excess paint, then continue to stipple.

Basics

Surface Preparation

If painting on wood, sand the surface until smooth, then wipe with a tack cloth to remove the dust. You can basecoat and seal the background in one step by mixing Multi-Purpose Sealer plus acrylic paint (2:1). Use either a sponge roller or the 1½" bristle bright to apply the basecoat. When dry, lightly sand with fine-grit sandpaper, then wipe again. Top with one or two more coats of paint with no sealer added, allowing adequate drying time between applications. It is important to have a smooth painting surface for when you apply the painting techniques.

If painting on tin, wash with equal parts of water and vinegar to clean, then rinse with water. Let dry, then basecoat as described above.

Transferring Patterns

Trace the pattern onto tracing paper. Take your time and use a ruler for straight lines. Position the traced pattern on top of the painting surface and secure with tape. Slide the transfer paper coated side down under the pattern, then lightly retrace the design using a stylus.

Finishing

Allow the paint to dry completely. Erase any visible graphite lines with a kneaded eraser. A varnish will bring the colors to life, but might also show any imperfections. To check for imperfections, lightly dampen the painting using the 1½" bristle bright and water. When dry, touch up areas as needed. Let dry. Spray with an even coat of matte Acrylic Sealer/Finisher. Once dry, top with another coat or two.

Watson's Flowers & Seeds

*T*his simple, yet effective, design features red dahlias amongst a spray of wildflowers.

Palette

◆ *DecoArt* Americana Acrylic Paint: Antique Gold Deep, Berry Red, Black Green, Burnt Orange, Cadmium Orange, Cadmium Yellow, Dark Chocolate, Deep Burgundy, Golden Straw, Hauser Light Green, Honey Brown, Khaki Tan, Lamp Black, Light Buttermilk, Napa Red, Navy Blue, Plantation Pine, Sea Breeze, Snow White
◆ *DecoArt* Americana Neons: Fiery Red

Brushes

◆ *Princeton:* Select Series 1½" bristle bright, Nos. 8 and 10 chisel blender, ⅛" and ⅝" deerfoot, No. 4 filbert, No. 10/0 liner, Nos. 1 and 3 round, No. 18/0 short liner, No. 10 old flared flat shader

Surface

◆ *Viking Woodcrafts* Wood Lid, No. 164-1048 (9" x 13"), and Wire Basket with Handles, No. 164-1047 (13" x 9" x 5½")

Other Supplies

◆ *Creative Imaginations* Impress-On rub-ons: Antique Accents, No. 28406; *DecoArt* Americana Acrylic Sealer/Finisher, Matte (spray); *DecoArt* Americana Multi-Purpose Sealer

Prep

1. Basecoat the lid using the sponge roller with Multi-Purpose Sealer + Khaki Tan (2:1). When dry, lightly sand and wipe to remove dust. Rebase with a coat of Khaki Tan with no sealer added. Let dry.

2. Apply a rub-on of choice to each corner of the lid. Apply a light wash of Khaki Tan over the rub-ons, placing mostly near the edges. Let dry.

3. Trace the pattern from page 68, and transfer a loose pattern for the flowers (just the outside edge for stippling the background) onto the lid. Use a ruler to apply the guidelines for the lettering.

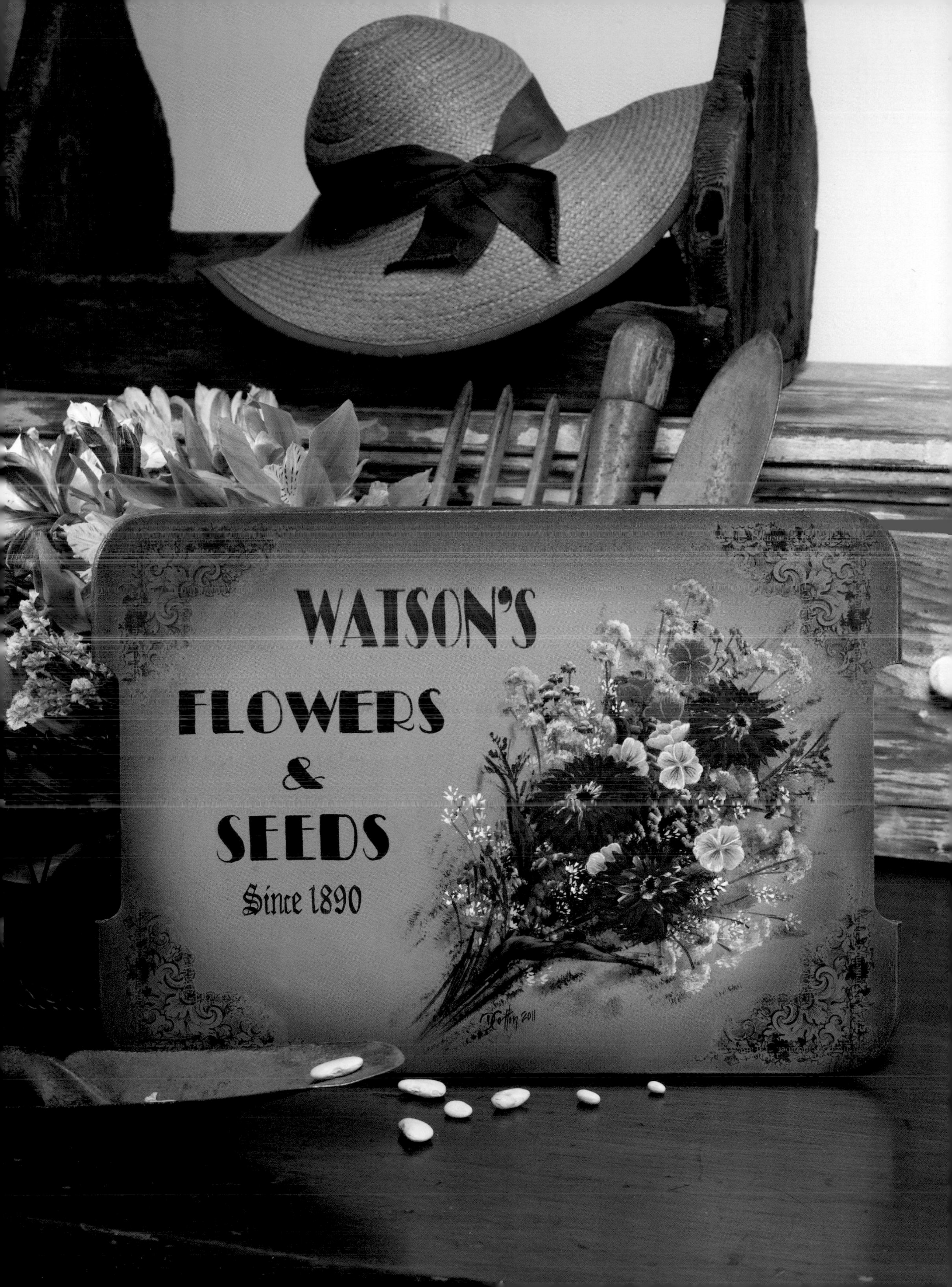
WATSON'S
FLOWERS
&
SEEDS
Since 1890

Paint

Note: When painting flowers, try to keep them natural looking by having them touch each other and overlap. Also vary the same flowers slightly in size and position and do not place them all facing in the same direction.

BACKGROUND

1. Lightly dampen the background area with water using the bristle bright. Use the 5/8" deerfoot with Plantation Pine to stipple the background, using both the flat part and the side of the brush to create different textures (**Fig. 1**).

2. Stipple the middle area with Black Green (**Fig. 2**).

3. Stipple the darkest areas with a touch of Lamp Black (**Fig. 3**).

DAHLIAS

1. Use the 1/8" deerfoot with Lamp Black to stipple the centers. Stipple Antique Gold Deep around the centers. Working wet on wet, use the dirty brush to pick up a small amount of Snow White, then stipple the highlights (**Fig. 4**).

2. Use the side of the filbert to create the petals. Start at the middle and pull outward, creating short V-shape strokes. Hold the brush vertically and always lead with the brightest color at the tip of the brush. Load one side of the brush with Berry Red and the other side with Cadmium Yellow. Apply the first row of petals around the center (**Fig. 4**).

3. As you work away from the center, the petals gradually darken in color. For the next darker value, use Berry Red and Cadmium Orange. Continue working around the flower, then pick up the next darker value of Berry Red and Deep Burgundy (**Fig. 5**).

4. The darkest petals on the outside are Napa Red. When dry, apply final highlights of Berry Red + Fiery Red (**Fig. 6**).

ALL LEAVES AND STEMS

1. Use the No. 3 round with Plantation Pine to base the leaves. Use the No. 10 chisel blender with Black Green to shade the bottoms and Hauser Light Green to highlight the tops. Float and chisel the color for a natural look.

2. Use the liner with Black Green to line the dahlia stems. Use the same brush with Dark Chocolate to line the stems for all filler flowers.

GOLD FILLER FLOWERS

1. Use the 1/8" deerfoot with Antique Gold Deep to stipple the gold filler flowers (**Fig. 7**). While still wet, pick up a touch of Snow White and lightly stipple highlights (**Fig. 8**).

2. Wipe the brush, pick up a touch of Dark Chocolate, then stipple lightly along the bottoms of the flowers (**Fig. 9**).

DARK BLUE FILLER FLOWERS

Note: Use the 1/8" deerfoot to create the dark blue filler flowers. When stippling, apply some flowers with just rounded tops and others in a circular motion so that they appear to have a center opening.

1. Touch the brush into Navy Blue, tip in Snow White, pounce once or twice on the palette to slightly blend, then stipple the flowers (**Fig. 10**).

LIGHT BLUE AND WHITE FILLER FLOWERS

1. Load the old flared flat shader with Sea Breeze, pounce on the palette to remove excess paint, then lightly dab on the surface to create the blossoms (**Fig. 11**). Clean the brush, load with Snow White, then repeat for the white filler flowers (**Fig. 12**).

YELLOW PANSIES

1. Base the pansies using the No. 1 round with Golden Straw. Use the No. 8 chisel blender with Honey Brown to shade near the centers (**Fig. 13**). Highlight the tips with Cadmium Yellow (**Fig. 14**).

2. Use the short liner with Light Buttermilk to lightly line around the outside edge to define the shape of the petals. Use the same color to pull fine lines inward from the tips of the petals. Line the veins with Berry Red (**Fig. 15**).

ORANGE PANSIES

1. Paint in the same manner as the yellow pansies. Basecoat with Burnt Orange, shade with Dark Chocolate, then highlight with Cadmium Orange.

2. Line the outside edges of the petals and pull fine lines inward from the tips of the petals with Cadmium Yellow. Add the veins with Berry Red.

LETTERING

Note: Refer to Tips & Techniques on page 10.

1. Use the liner with Berry Red to letter "WATSON'S".

Skip a line of Fiery Red through the middle of the Berry Red letters.

2. Use the liner with Lamp Black to letter "FLOWERS & SEEDS".

3. Use the short liner with Lamp Black to letter "since 1890".

Finish

1. Antique the outside edge as described in Tips & Techniques on page 10.

2. When dry, spray with Sealer/Finisher. Let dry.

Fig. 1   Fig. 2   Fig. 3

Fig. 4   Fig. 5   Fig. 6

Fig. 7   Fig. 8   Fig. 9

Fig. 10   Fig. 11   Fig. 12

Fig. 13   Fig. 14   Fig. 15

Aunt Bea's Antiques

There are many vintage pieces of enamelware, including coffee pots, strainers, sauce pans, chamber pots, jugs, and pitchers. This particular pitcher is very elegant due to its curved shape. Enamelware is porcelain enamel-covered iron and is very lightweight and easy to clean. Unlike cast-iron cookware, enamelware does not react with acidic foods.

Palette

◆ *DecoArt* Americana Acrylic Paint: Berry Red, Black Green, Cadmium Orange, Cadmium Yellow, Camel, Charcoal Grey, Citron Green, Hauser Dark Green, Hauser Light Green, Hauser Medium Green, Lamp Black, Light Buttermilk, Milk Chocolate, Napa Red, Neutral Grey, Payne's Grey, Snow White, Traditional Burnt Sienna

Brushes

◆ *Princeton:* Select Series 1½" bristle bright, No. 8 chisel blender, ⅛" and ⅝" deerfoot, ⅜" lunar blender, ½" lunar mop, No. 0 round, No. 1 script liner, No. 10/0 short liner; Umbria Series No. 12 flat

Surface

◆ *Simply Cotton* Tin Sign (12½" x 9½")

Other Supplies

◆ *Creative Imaginations* Impress-On rub-ons: Antique Accents, No. 28406; *DecoArt* Americana Acrylic Sealer/Finisher, Matte (spray); *DecoArt* Americana Multi-Purpose Sealer

Prep

1. Wipe the tin sign with a mix of water and vinegar (1:1). Rinse with clear water and let dry. Basecoat using the sponge roller with Multi-Purpose Sealer + Light Buttermilk (2:1). When dry, lightly sand and wipe to remove dust. Rebase with two coats of Light Buttermilk with no sealer added, allowing adequate drying time between applications.

2. Trace the pattern from page 69, and transfer the main pattern lines onto the sign. Transfer details as needed.

Paint

Note: Refer to the pattern for placement of shading and highlights.

BACKGROUND

Note: Use painter's tape to mask each section of the background as you work to maintain clean edges. The bottom section is darkest and gradually lightens as you work toward the top.

1. Begin with the middle area of the floor. Use painter's tape to mask above and below this area. Use the bristle bright with water to slightly dampen the surface. Use the 5/8" deerfoot to stipple the middle area with Neutral Grey. Use the lunar mop to soften the edges. When dry, redampen the surface, then stipple with Charcoal Grey, covering a narrower area. Mop to soften. Remove tape and let dry thoroughly.

2. Use the same technique to apply the top and bottom sections, first with Neutral Grey and then with Charcoal Grey. Keep in mind that the bottom section is the darkest.

3. Use the bristle bright to dampen the shaded areas along both sides and by the base of the pitcher. Use the No. 12 flat with Lamp Black to float the shading, keeping it narrow. Mop to soften.

PITCHER

1. Touch up the Light Buttermilk basecoat, if needed.

2. Use the No. 12 flat with Neutral Grey to shade the outside edges, keeping it fairly wide. Mop to soften. Use the chisel blender with Neutral Grey to shade under the top rim and along the bottom of the pitcher. Deepen shaded areas with a small amount of Lamp Black (**Fig. 1**).

3. Use the lunar blender to drybrush Snow White highlights through the top middle area of the pitcher (**Fig. 2**).

4. Use the lunar blender to apply Camel tints to the top left, top right, right middle, and bottom areas of the pitcher. Clean the brush, dry, then apply soft Berry Red tints to the top left, bottom left, and right area of the pitcher (**Fig. 3**).

5. Apply the chipped areas using the short liner with Lamp Black (**Fig. 1**). Use the chisel blender to float Milk Chocolate around the chips to age. Further age with tints of Cadmium Orange (**Fig. 2**).

6. Line the rim and handle using the script liner with Payne's Grey (**Fig. 1**). Use the chisel blender and Lamp Black to shade along the outside edges of the handle and along the top and bottom of the rim (**Fig. 2**). Apply rust spots to the handle using the No. 0 round with Traditional Burnt Sienna (**Fig. 2**).

7. Use the short liner to skip Light Buttermilk highlights on the middle of the rim and handle, then brighten with Snow White. Add the screw just below where the rim and handle meet with Payne's Grey, then detail with Snow White (**Fig. 3**).

GERBERA DAISIES

Note: Paint each daisy petal individually using the No. 0 round with a wet-on-wet technique. The medium value is Berry Red, the dark value is Napa Red, the darkest value (where one petal lays behind another) is Napa Red + a touch of Payne's Grey, and the light value is Cadmium Yellow. Use the paint sparingly so that one color does not dominate another. Once you apply the color, wipe the brush on a paper towel to remove excess paint, then slightly blend the colors where they meet.

1. Apply Napa Red at the base of the petal. Wipe excess paint on a paper towel, pick up Berry Red, then paint the rest of the petal. Wipe the brush on a paper towel, pick up Cadmium Yellow, then streak the top area of the petal. Wipe the brush. If an extra dark value is needed, pick up Napa Red + a touch of Payne's Grey, and blend in the darkest area (**Fig. 1**).

2. Use the 1/8" deerfoot to stipple Berry Red in the middle section of the large daisy. While wet, stipple the middle area and around the outside edge with a touch of Napa Red (**Fig. 1**), then deepen with Napa Red + a touch of Payne's Grey (**Fig. 2**). When dry, add highlight strokes using the short liner with Cadmium Orange, then brighten with Cadmium Yellow. Add a final highlight of Snow White (**Fig. 3**).

3. A small section of the middle of the top right daisy is also visible. Paint this area in the same manner as the middle section of the large daisy, but place the darkest values on the bottom and the lightest values on the top.

4. If you need to create more separation between the petals or clean up any edges, use the chisel blender to float and chisel with Lamp Black (**Fig. 2**).

5. Add more highlights using the short liner with Cadmium Yellow, particularly to the large daisy in the center, which is the brightest. Add the brightest highlights with Snow White (**Fig. 3**).

DAISY STEMS

1. Paint the stems using the No. 0 round with Hauser Medium Green. Switch to the liner when basing the part of the stem that meets the flower.

2. Use the chisel blender with Hauser Dark Green to shade the stems along the bottom side and where they meet the pitcher, then deepen with Black Green.

3. Highlight the tops with Hauser Light Green, then brighten with a touch of Citron Green.

4. Using the short liner, skim Hauser Dark Green between the leaves, then darken with Black Green.

5. Highlight the tips and middle areas of the leaves with Hauser Light Green. Add the brightest highlights with Citron Green.

LETTERING

Note: Refer to Tips & Techniques on page 10.

Use the short liner with Payne's Grey to letter "Aunt Bea's ANTIQUES".

Finish

1. Embellish the corners and top center of the sign using the desired Antique Accents rub-ons.

2. To age the sign, dampen the edges with water. Use the 1/8" deerfoot with Lamp Black to stipple the sides of the sign. Mop to soften. Use the lunar blender with Berry Red to softly drybrush tints in the corners, under the large center daisy, under the top part of the handle, and the left middle area of the pitcher.

3. When dry, spray with Sealer/Finisher. Let dry.

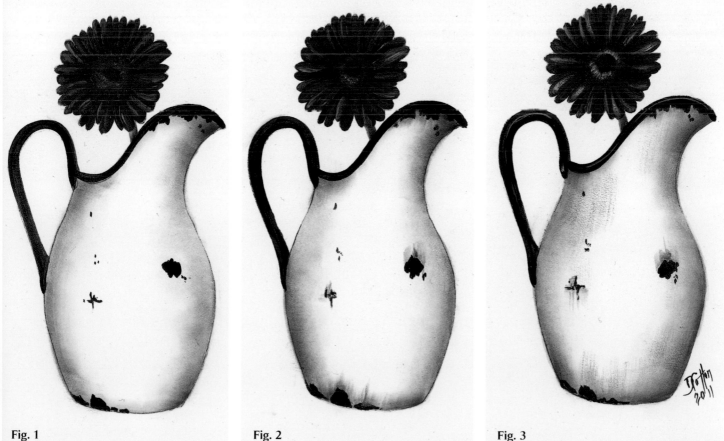

Fig. 1

Fig. 2

Fig. 3

Winchester's Orange Spice Tea

*O*range spice tea contains either orange zest or dried orange peel. It is generally blended with black tea leaves to form the base, to which a combination of spices can be added, such as cloves, cinnamon, and nutmeg.

Palette

◆ *DecoArt* Americana Acrylic Paint: Burnt Orange, Cadmium Orange, Cadmium Yellow, Dark Chocolate, Driftwood, Hauser Medium Green, Heritage Brick, Honey Brown, Jack-O'-Lantern Orange, Lamp Black, Light Buttermilk, Milk Chocolate, Moon Yellow, Payne's Grey, Primary Red, Snow White, Soft Black, Tangerine
◆ *DecoArt* Americana Neons: Fiery Red

Brushes

◆ *Princeton:* Select Series 1½" bristle bright, No. 10 chisel blender, ¼" and ⅜" deerfoot, No. 10 filbert, No. 10/0 liner, ⅜" lunar blender, ½" lunar mop, No. 1 script liner, No. 10/0 short liner; Synthetic Sable 1½" flat wash; Umbria Series No. 12 flat

Surface

◆ *JB Wood Products* Arch Plaque, No. 0180 (10" x 10")

Other Supplies

◆ *DecoArt* Americana Acrylic Sealer/Finisher, Matte (spray); *DecoArt* Americana Multi-Purpose Sealer; airtight container

Prep

1. Lightly sand and wipe to remove dust.

2. Create a Light Yellow Mix of Snow White + Moon Yellow (2:1) and place in an airtight container to use throughout the project. Basecoat the plaque using the sponge roller with Multi-Purpose Sealer + Light Yellow Mix (2:1). When dry, lightly sand and wipe to remove dust. Rebase with the Light Yellow Mix with no sealer added. Let dry. Use the filbert to base the routed edge with Heritage Brick.

3. For an aged look, drybrush the routed edge using the lunar blender with Lamp Black, dragging the brush vertically along the edges. Add random tints of Primary Red.

4. Trace the pattern from page 70, and transfer the main pattern lines onto the plaque. Transfer details as needed.

WINCHESTER'S

ORANGE
SPICE
TEA

Kettle Co

1854

Cotton 2011

Paint

Note: Refer to the pattern for placement of shading and highlights.

BACKGROUND

Note: The background has an aged, weathered appearance.

1. Use the 1¹/2" flat wash with Honey Brown to shade around the outside edge of the plaque. Use the lunar mop to soften (**Fig. 1**).

2. Dampen the outside edge with water using the bristle bright. Use the ³/8" deerfoot to stipple around the outside edge with Milk Chocolate. Mop to soften. Let dry. Repeat with Dark Chocolate, covering a narrower area, and let dry. Repeat with Soft Black, covering an even narrower area. Use the No. 12 flat with Lamp Black to shade around the outside edge (**Fig. 2**).

3. Use the ³/8" deerfoot to stipple Cadmium Yellow highlights on the center area of the plaque. Apply tints with Jack-O'-Lantern Orange. Add Soft Black cracks with the short liner. Use the script liner to apply a Lamp Black pinstripe border ¹/4" in from the routed edge (**Fig. 3**).

ORANGE

1. The basecoat color of the orange is the Light Yellow Mix. Touch up, if necessary. Dampen the surface with a small amount of water using the bristle bright. Use the ¹/4" deerfoot with Cadmium Yellow to stipple the highlights. Mop to soften. Let dry. Apply Snow White highlights in the same manner (**Fig. 1**).

2. Use the ¹/4" deerfoot to stipple the outside edge with Tangerine. When dry, stipple with Jack-O'-Lantern Orange (**Fig. 2**).

3. Use the chisel blender to softly shade Cadmium Orange along the bottom and top outside edge, then deepen slightly with Heritage Brick. Add the navel using the short liner with Dark Chocolate, then highlight with Snow White. Line the creases in the orange skin with Jack-O'-Lantern Orange. Use the ¹/4" deerfoot to lightly stipple Hauser Medium Green on the top middle area of the orange to accent (**Fig. 3**).

ORANGE WEDGE

1. Base the rind using the filbert with Cadmium Yellow. While still wet, use the liner to line the top with Tangerine, the middle with Jack-O'-Lantern Orange, and the bottom with Heritage Brick (**Fig. 1**).

2. Use the liner with Cadmium Yellow to line the wedge, working from the top down and the bottom up. Line the highlights with Snow White to create the segments (**Fig. 2**).

3. Use the chisel blender to add shading between the segments with Tangerine and Jack-O'-Lantern Orange. Use the same brush with Burnt Orange to shade between the sections, working from the bottom and chiseling up the sides. Deepen with Heritage Brick (**Fig. 3**).

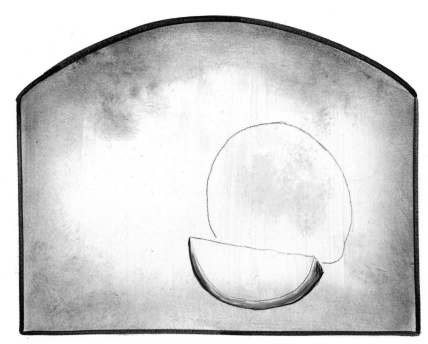

Fig. 1

KETTLE

1. Base the kettle using the filbert with Light Buttermilk. Use the 1¹/₂" flat wash to shade the outside edges with Driftwood. Slightly deepen the shading first with Soft Black and then with Lamp Black.

2. Slightly dampen the surface with water. Use the ³/₈" deerfoot to stipple Snow White highlights.

3. Use the chisel blender with the Light Yellow Mix to apply tints to the top left of the kettle, below the label, to the bottom right of the kettle, and to the lid. Tint the top left and bottom right areas with Jack-O'-Lantern Orange.

4. Use the liner with Payne's Grey to apply the rim, spout, top of the lid, and handle. Skip Lamp Black along the bottom of the kettle. Line Snow White highlights on the bottom rim, top rim, and handle rims. Apply areas of chipped paint with Lamp Black. Use the chisel blender to float and chisel rust around the chipped areas and on the bottom of the kettle with Milk Chocolate and Burnt Orange.

LABEL ON KETTLE

1. Base the label using the filbert with the Light Yellow Mix. Use the chisel blender to shade the outside edge of the label with Milk Chocolate, then deepen with Soft Black. Add tints with Jack-O'-Lantern Orange.

2. Use the short liner with Lamp Black to apply the "Kettle Co." lettering and "1854" date and to outline the label. (See Tips & Techniques on page 10.)

3. Use the chisel blender to loosely shade Soft Black around the outside edge of the label.

LETTERING

Note: Refer to Tips & Techniques on page 10.

1. Use the short liner with Heritage Brick to letter "WINCHESTER'S", then skip Fiery Red through the center of each letter to brighten.

2. Use the same brush with Lamp Black to letter "ORANGE SPICE TEA."

Finish

When dry, spray with Acrylic Sealer/Finisher. Let dry.

Fig. 2

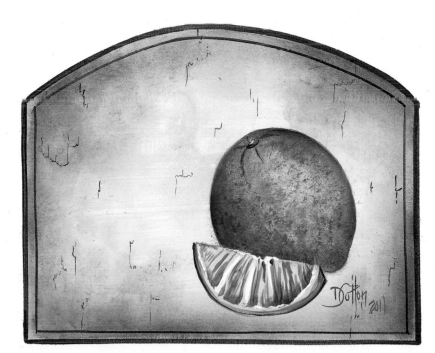

Fig. 3

Greenfield Carriage Co.

*I*magine traveling down an old wagon trail. Horse-drawn vehicles have been around for thousands of years. In past centuries, farm wagons were pulled by teams of oxen, mules, or horses.

Palette

◆ *DecoArt* Americana Acrylic Paint: Antique Maroon, Avocado Dip, Black Green, Cadmium Orange, Cadmium Yellow, Dark Chocolate, Dioxazine Purple, Golden Straw, Hauser Dark Green, Hauser Light Green, Hauser Medium Green, Heritage Brick, Honey Brown, Jack-O'-Lantern Orange, Khaki Tan, Lamp Black, Light Buttermilk, Milk Chocolate, Sea Breeze, Snow White, Soft Black, True Red, Tuscan Red

Brushes

◆ *Princeton:* Select Series ⅛" angular shader, No. 10 chisel blender, ⅛" and ¼" deerfoot, Nos. 2 and 6 filbert, ⅛" filbert grainer, ½" flat wash, No. 10/0 liner, ½" lunar mop, No. 0 round, No. 1 script liner, No. 10/0 short liner; old flared No. 8 flat shader; Umbria Series No. 12 flat

Surface

◆ *Simply Cotton* Tin Sign (12½" x 9½")

Other Supplies

◆ *DecoArt* Americana Acrylic Sealer/Finisher, Matte (spray); *DecoArt* Americana Multi-Purpose Sealer; *Winsor & Newton* Winton Oil Colour: Raw Umber; odorless thinner; circular item (optional, for painting wheels)

Prep

1. Wipe the tin sign with a mix of water and vinegar (1:1). Rinse with clear water and let dry. Basecoat using the sponge roller with Multi-Purpose Sealer + Khaki Tan (2:1). When dry, lightly sand and wipe to remove dust. Rebase with two coats of Khaki Tan with no sealer added, allowing adequate drying time between each application.

2. Measure and mark a 1/4" border along all sides. Apply painter's tape along the border for a clean edge, then base using the No. 6 filbert with Lamp Black. When dry, remove tape. Apply a 1/8" pinstripe along the border using the script liner with Heritage Brick. Let dry.

3. Trace the pattern from page 71, and transfer the main pattern lines for the cart and lettering onto the sign. Transfer details as needed.

Paint

WAGON

1. Tape off so you can work on one board at a time, and paint using a wet-on-wet technique. Base the board using the No. 6 filbert with Honey Brown. To create the wood grain, use the filbert grainer to streak the board with Milk Chocolate. Next, streak with Dark Chocolate, keeping it toward the edges. Finally, streak with a small amount of Golden Straw, keeping it in the center. Repeat for all boards.

2. Use the 1/2" flat wash with Milk Chocolate to shade the ends of the cart on the front and side. Use the lunar mop to soften. Use the chisel blender with Dark Chocolate to deepen the shading, then add the deepest shading with Soft Black; note that the darkest area is the front of the cart.

3. Line the boards and wood grain with Lamp Black. Add the nails using the short liner with Soft Black. When dry, loosely shade around the nails with Lamp Black. Highlight the nails with Light Buttermilk.

GROUND AREA

1. Apply painter's tape to the top of the ground area for a clean edge. Use the No. 12 flat to float the grass with Hauser Dark Green. Mop to soften. Deepen with Black Green. Mop to soften.

WHEELS

Note: Paint the shaft and wheels in the following order: right wheels, shaft, left wheels. If desired, use a circular item, such as a bottle cap, as a guide when painting the wheels.

1. Use the script liner with Lamp Black to apply the outer rim of the wheel. Paint the inner rim and spokes with Dark Chocolate. Each spoke is narrow at the ends and wider through the middle. To apply, start on the tip of the brush and apply pressure as you pull so the spoke becomes wider through the center, then release pressure so it becomes narrow at the end.

2. Shade both ends of the spokes using the chisel blender with Soft Black. Highlight the middle with Honey Brown. Use the same color to highlight the tops of the inner rims. Line the shafts with Lamp Black.

RED FLOWERS

1. Stipple the background greenery using the 1/4" deerfoot with Hauser Dark Green, then deepen with Black Green (**Fig. 1**).

2. Apply the stems using the short liner with Hauser Light Green (**Fig. 2**).

3. Load the 1/8" deerfoot with Antique Maroon, tip in True Red, pounce on the palette to blend, then stipple the blossoms (**Fig. 3**).

TOPIARY TREE

1. Use the short liner with Milk Chocolate to line the trunk. While still wet, shade the left side with Lamp Black. Use the filbert grainer to stipple the greenery with Hauser Dark Green, then deepen with Black Green (**Fig. 4**).

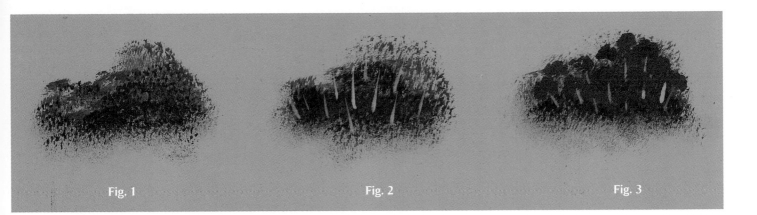

Fig. 1

Fig. 2

Fig. 3

Fig. 4

Fig. 5

Fig. 6

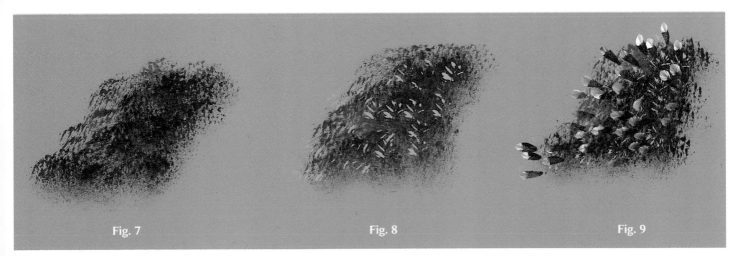

Fig. 7

Fig. 8

Fig. 9

2. Stipple with touches of Hauser Medium Green and Hauser Light Green (**Fig. 5**).

3. Stipple the top with Avocado Dip and the bottom with Sea Breeze. Add touches of Lamp Black using the tip of the filbert grainer (**Fig. 6**).

PURPLE FLOWERS
1. Use the 1/4" deerfoot to stipple the greenery with Hauser Dark Green and Black Green (**Fig. 7**).

2. Use the old flared flat shader with Sea Breeze to stipple the bluish greenery (**Fig. 8**).

3. Load the angular shader with Dioxazine Purple, tip in Snow White, lightly pounce on palette to blend, then touch the surface to create the purple buds (**Fig. 9**).

RED TIN
1. Base with the No. 6 filbert and Heritage Brick. Use the chisel blender to shade the left front, bottom edge, left side, and under the rim with Antique Maroon. Use the same brush to highlight the front right side and through the middle with Tuscan Red. Use the short liner with Soft Black to add a few dents and cracks.

2. Line the "T J TINS" lettering using the short liner with Golden Straw. (See Tips & Techniques on page 10.)

WHITE FLOWERS IN TIN
1. Use the 1/4" deerfoot to stipple the greenery with Hauser Dark Green, then deepen with Black Green (**Fig. 10**).

2. Load the No. 0 round with Hauser Dark Green, tip in Hauser Light Green, then stroke the leaves (**Fig. 11**).

3. Use the No. 2 filbert to create the hydrangea-style blossoms. Touch the side of the brush into Avocado Dip, tip in Snow White, then stroke on tiny petals. Brighten the tops with Snow White (**Fig. 12**).

WHITE FLOWERS CASCADING OVER WAGON
1. Use the 1/4" deerfoot to stipple the greenery with Hauser Dark Green and Hauser Medium Green (**Fig. 13**).

2. Load the old flared flat shader with Sea Breeze and stipple the bluish greenery (**Fig. 14**).

3. Line the stems with Snow White. Load the 1/8" deerfoot with Snow White and touch to the surface to create the tiny white flowers. Load the same brush with Dark Chocolate, tip in Snow White, blend lightly on the palette, then touch on the remaining flowers (**Fig. 15**).

BUCKET
1. Use the No. 6 filbert with Light Buttermilk to base the bucket. Shade the outside edges and along the bottom using the chisel blender with Soft Black. Mop to soften. Use the chisel blender to drybrush highlights with Snow White.

2. Create the chipped areas on the bucket using the short liner with Lamp Black.

3. Line the top rim using the short liner with Tuscan Red, then highlight with Snow White. Line the metal handle with Lamp Black. Use the short liner with Milk Chocolate to add the wooden hand grip, then while still wet, line Lamp Black along the bottom and Golden Straw along the top.

ORANGE TULIPS IN BUCKET
1. Use the 1/4" deerfoot to stipple greenery at the base first with Hauser Dark Green and then with Black Green (**Fig. 16**).

2. Use the short liner to pull the leaves with Hauser Dark Green and Hauser Medium Green (**Fig. 17**).

3. Stroke the tulips using the round with Cadmium Orange. While still wet, stroke the highlights with Cadmium Yellow and Jack-O'-Lantern Orange. Place a touch of Black Green on the top inside edges. Use the 1/8" deerfoot to stipple a touch of Hauser Medium Green at the bottoms of the tulips (**Fig. 18**).

LETTERING
Note: Refer to Tips & Techniques on page 10.

1. Use the liner with Heritage Brick to letter "GREENFIELD CARRIAGE CO." Skip a line of Tuscan Red through the middle each letter.

2. Use the short liner with Heritage Brick to letter "For All Of Your Hauling Needs".

Finish

1. Antique as described in Tips & Techniques on page 10.

2. When dry, spray with Sealer/Finisher. Let dry.

Fig. 10

Fig. 11

Fig. 12

Fig. 13

Fig. 14

Fig. 15

Fig. 16

Fig. 17

Fig. 18

Sunnyside Feeds & Needs Co.

When a rooster finds food, he calls the hens to eat first. He does this by sounding a high-pitch cluck, as well as by picking up and dropping the food. Hens cluck loudly after laying eggs and to call their chicks.

Palette

◆ *DecoArt* Americana Acrylic Paint: Antique Maroon, Antique Rose, Black Green, Bluegrass Green, Burnt Orange, Cadmium Orange, Cadmium Yellow, Charcoal Grey, Dark Chocolate, Driftwood, Golden Straw, Honey Brown, Lamp Black, Light Buttermilk, Marigold, Milk Chocolate, Moon Yellow, Navy Blue, Payne's Grey, Snow White, Soft Black, Traditional Burnt Sienna, True Blue, True Red, Tuscan Red

Brushes

◆ *Princeton:* Select Series 1½" bristle bright, Nos. 4 and 10 chisel blender, ¼" deerfoot, No. 6 filbert, ½" flat wash, No. 10/0 liner, ½" lunar mop, ¼" lunar blender, No. 3 round, No. 1 script liner, No. 18/0 short liner; Umbria Series No. 12 flat

Surface

◆ *JB Wood Products* Market Sign Board, No. 0804A (16" x 21" x 1½")

Other Supplies

◆ *DecoArt* Americana Acrylic Sealer/Finisher, Matte (spray); *DecoArt* Americana Multi-Purpose Sealer

Prep

1. Lightly sand the sign board and wipe to remove dust. Basecoat using the sponge roller with Multi-Purpose Sealer + Lamp Black (2:1). When dry, rebase with Lamp Black with no sealer added. Let dry.

2. Use painter's tape to mask the top and bottom sections of the board to keep them clean as you work on the middle background area.

3. *Background.* The background is painted to resemble barn boards. Measure and mark the barn boards at the top and bottom of middle section of the sign board 2¼" apart. Use painter's tape to mask the boards, as you will be painting them one at a time. Fold an edge of the tape over for easy removal. As you work, leave a ¹/₁₆" line of the black background showing through for the board line, then tape off and continue to paint the next board.

4. Use the flat wash on both the flat and chisel edges for streaking through colors. Randomly streak through the following colors, referring to the color photo for placement: Dark Chocolate, Driftwood, Charcoal Grey, Honey Brown, Milk Chocolate, Soft Black, and a small amount of Lamp Black. Be careful not to overblend the colors, as they will turn muddy and you will not achieve the look you want.

5. Use the script liner with Lamp Black to apply the wood grain. Use the same color to touch up the black board lines, if needed.

6. With the No. 10 chisel blender, float and chisel in Driftwood, Honey Brown, and Lamp Black to enhance the boards. Apply these colors against some of the wood grain lines and also randomly along the outside edges of the boards.

7. Trace the pattern from page 72, and transfer the main pattern lines onto the background. Transfer details as needed.

Paint

Note: When painting the chickens, begin with those in the back of the design and work toward the front.

ROOSTER AND ALL HENS

1. *Beaks.* (**Note:** The beaks are painted wet on wet; work on one beak at a time.) Base the beak using the No. 3 round and Honey Brown (**Fig. 1**). While still wet, shade with Traditional Burnt Sienna (**Fig. 2**) and highlight with Marigold (**Fig. 3**). Use the short liner with Honey Brown to create the nostril (**Fig. 2**). Detail with Lamp Black and highlight with Marigold (**Fig. 3**).

2. *Eyes.* Dot the eyes with Marigold. Use the No. 3 round to wash the eyes with Burnt Orange (**Fig. 4**). Apply smaller dots of Lamp Black for the pupils. Use the short liner with Lamp Black to line around the outside edge of the Marigold dot (**Fig. 5**). Highlight with Light Buttermilk (**Fig. 6**).

3. *Ears.* Each hen has an ear near each eye. Base the ear with using the No. 3 round with Honey Brown (**Fig. 1**). While still wet, shade the bottom of the ear with a touch of Traditional Burnt Sienna (**Fig. 2**), then highlight the top with Light Buttermilk (**Fig. 3**).

4. *Legs and feet.* Base the legs and feet using the No. 3 round with Honey Brown. Float and chisel the shading using the No. 4 chisel blender with Dark Chocolate (**Fig. 7**), then deepen some areas with Soft Black. Shade along the tops of the legs just under the feathers with Soft Black (**Fig. 8**). Highlight with Golden Straw. Apply the claws using the short liner with Soft Black, then line highlights with Light Buttermilk (**Fig. 9**).

5. *Combs and wattles.* Base the combs and wattles using the No. 3 round with Antique Rose. Use the No. 4 chisel blender with Tuscan Red to apply shading (**Fig. 1**), then deepen with a brush mix of Tuscan Red + a touch of Black Green (**Fig. 2**). Highlight with a brush mix of Antique Rose + Light Buttermilk. Add random tints with True Red (**Fig. 3**).

ROOSTER

1. Use the filbert to base the neck feathers with Moon Yellow and the breast feathers with Burnt Orange. Use the No. 4 chisel blender to chisel Burnt Orange through the neck feathers, working from the top down and the bottom up,

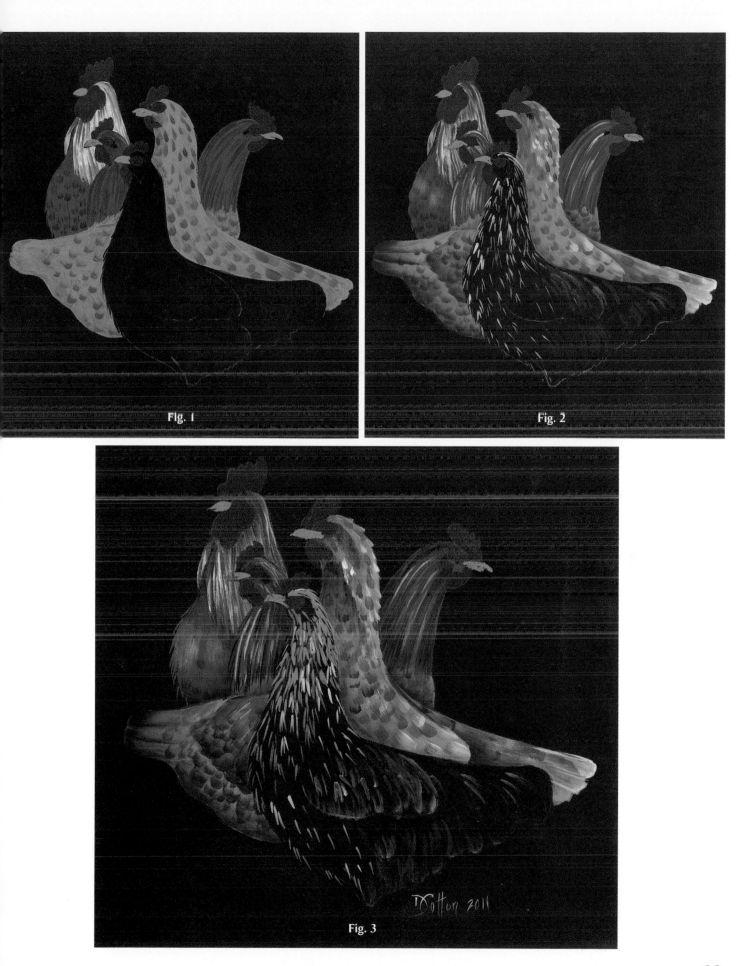

Fig. 1

Fig. 2

Fig. 3

allowing some of the Moon Yellow base to show through near the front (**Fig. 1**). Apply more color with chisels of Traditional Burnt Sienna (**Fig. 2**). Shade around the wattle, against Hen No. 1's head, and on the top and bottom of the right neck feathers with Black Green (**Fig. 3**).

2. Use the filbert with Black Green to apply the C-stroke feathers on the breast. To do this, slightly thin the paint with a touch of water, load the brush, then gently fan the brush out on the palette. Touch the tip of the brush onto the painting surface and pull small C-strokes to create the tiny feathers. Practice this a few times on your palette before moving to your surface (**Fig. 1**). Shade the top and bottom and against Hen No. 1 using the No. 10 chisel blender with Black Green. Use the lunar blender to drybrush Light Buttermilk highlights on the breast (**Fig. 2**). Loosely wash Cadmium Orange and Cadmium Yellow over the highlight areas with the No. 10 chisel blender. Use the short liner to pull tiny Burnt Orange feathers on the front edge of the breast. Slightly deepen the Black Green shaded areas using the No. 10 chisel blender with Lamp Black (**Fig. 3**).

HEN NO. 1 (CLOSEST TO ROOSTER)

1. Basecoat the neck feathers using the filbert with Burnt Orange. Base the breast area with Honey Brown. Use the No. 4 chisel blender to chisel the neck feathers with Traditional Burnt Sienna (**Fig. 1**), then with Marigold and Cadmium Orange (**Fig. 2**). Add some darker feathers toward the middle and back with Antique Maroon, then slightly deepen with Lamp Black (**Fig. 3**).

2. Shade the breast area where it meets the other hen using the No. 4 chisel blender with Dark Chocolate (**Fig. 2**). Slightly deepen with a touch of Black Green (**Fig. 3**).

HEN NO. 2

1. Use the No. 10 chisel blender with Traditional Burnt Sienna to apply the neck feathers (**Fig. 1**). Add more feathers with Marigold, Burnt Orange, and Cadmium Orange (**Fig. 2**). Add the darker feathers with Antique Maroon and Lamp Black. Shade around the wattle and against Hen No. 3 with Antique Maroon, then deepen with Lamp Black (**Fig. 3**).

2. Use the filbert to base the body with a loose coat of Honey Brown. Use the No. 4 chisel blender with Burnt Orange to paint small C-strokes for the feathers (**Fig. 1**). Apply more feathers with Traditional Burnt Sienna and Antique Maroon (**Fig. 2**). Deepen further with Soft Black (**Fig. 3**).

3. Use the No. 10 chisel blender to float and chisel the tail feathers and wing with Soft Black. Use the same color to shade along the bottom of the breast and against both hens (**Fig. 2**). Deepen the shading on the tail feathers and wing with Lamp Black. Apply tints along the top near the tail, on the wing, and on the front of the breast with Burnt Orange and Marigold (**Fig. 3**).

HEN NO. 3

1. This hen is a bit brighter than the one behind it and the feathers are painted very loosely. Base the body and neck using the filbert with Honey Brown. Note that the feathers are larger near the tail and gradually become smaller as you work up the neck. When painting the feathers on the neck, use the filbert on the chisel edge. Apply C-stroke feathers with Milk Chocolate and Dark Chocolate (**Fig. 1**). Apply the brighter feathers with a brush mix of Honey Brown + Light Buttermilk (**Fig. 2**).

2. Use the No. 10 chisel blender with Dark Chocolate to shade near the front of the neck and against the wing on the body (**Fig. 2**). Deepen the neck front and behind the wing with Soft Black. Use the filbert to add a few Soft Black C-strokes in the darker areas. Use the No. 10 chisel blender to brighten the tops of the neck, wing, and tail with tints of Burnt Orange, Cadmium Orange, and Cadmium Yellow (**Fig. 3**).

HEN NO. 4

1. Use the filbert with Payne's Grey to apply a loose basecoat. Use the No. 4 chisel blender to float and chisel Navy Blue on the tail, top of wing, and thigh. Use the same brush to chisel Lamp Black on the neck and to pull some tiny Lamp Black feathers on the front breast (**Fig. 1**).

2. Brighten the top of the tail and wing using the No. 4 chisel blender with True Blue and Bluegrass Green. Apply Marigold feathers with the liner.

Note that there are more feathers on the neck and less feathers as you move down on the body (**Fig. 2**). Apply more feathers on the neck and top of the head with Honey Brown. Softly float and chisel Marigold along the bottom of the wing to help separate it from the breast, bottom of the thigh, and tail (**Fig. 3**).

FEED BINS

1. These are painted to resemble galvanized bins. Tape off the outside edge of each bin as you work to achieve clean, straight lines and paint the bins individually, working wet on wet. To begin, use the deerfoot to stipple with Driftwood. While still wet, stipple shading on the bottom with Charcoal Grey. Stipple highlights with Snow White. Use the flat wash to shade the darker areas with Lamp Black.

2. Use the deerfoot to stipple the rust spots. Begin with the darkest color and continue, gradually increasing coverage with each additional color. Stipple the rust spots with a small amount of Lamp Black, then with Traditional Burnt Umber, and finally with Burnt Orange.

FINAL SHADING

1. Slightly dampen the areas to be shaded prior to applying color using the bristle bright. Use the No. 12 flat with Lamp Black to shade around the outside edge of the painting surface. This is applied over the left ends of the bins and across the bottom. Use the same color to shade to the left of the rooster, under all the chickens' bodies, to the right of Hen No. 2, and under the tail feathers of Hen No. 4. Use the lunar mop to soften.

2. Use the No. 12 flat to float Tuscan Red around the outside edges of the top and bottom boards where the lettering will be applied. Mop to soften.

LETTERING

Note: Refer to Tips & Techniques on page 10.

1. Use the liner with Honey Brown to letter "SUNNYSIDE FEEDS & NEEDS CO".

2. Shade the top and bottom of each letter using the No. 10 chisel blender with Milk Chocolate.

Finish

When dry, spray with Sealer/Finisher. Let dry.

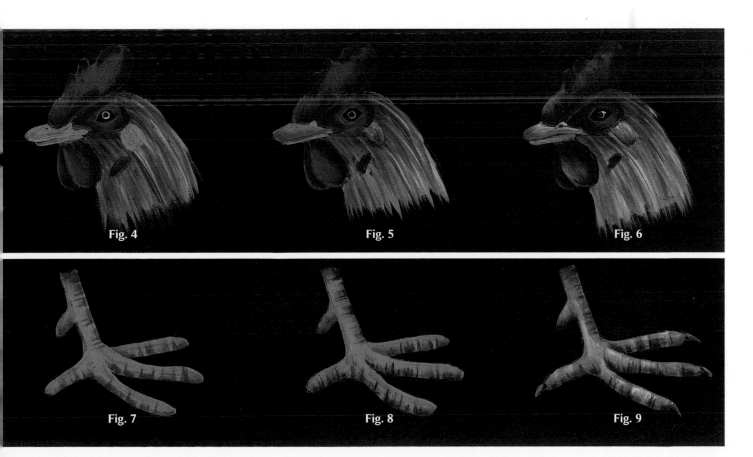

Fig. 4   Fig. 5   Fig. 6

Fig. 7   Fig. 8   Fig. 9

New York Kennel Club

The very first kennel club was formed in England in 1873. The first show was held at the Crystal Palace and featured 975 entries. Nearly eleven years later, in 1884, the American Kennel Club was formed.

Palette

◆ *DecoArt* Americana Acrylic Paint: Antique White, Black Plum, Burnt Orange, Charcoal Grey, Cocoa, Dark Chocolate, Driftwood, Evergreen, Gooseberry Pink, Lamp Black, Light Buttermilk, Milk Chocolate, Shading Flesh, Slate Grey, Snow White, Soft Black, White Wash

Brushes

◆ *Princeton:* Select Series 1½" bristle bright, Nos. 6 and 10 chisel blender, Nos. 4 and 6 filbert, ¼" filbert grainer, No. 10/0 liner, Nos. 1 and 3 round, No. 18/0 short liner; Umbria Series No. 12 flat

Surface

◆ *Simply Cotton* Tin Sign (12½" x 9½")

Other Supplies

◆ *DecoArt* Americana Acrylic Sealer/Finisher, Matte (spray); *DecoArt* Americana Multi-Purpose Sealer; *Winsor & Newton* Winton Oil Colour: Raw Umber; odorless thinner

New York Kennel Club

Breeding
Champions
Since 1898

Prep

1. Wipe the tin sign with a mix of water and vinegar (1:1). Rinse with clear water and let dry.

2. Basecoat using the sponge roller with Multi-Purpose Sealer + White Wash (2:1). When dry, lightly sand and wipe to remove dust. Rebase with two coats of White Wash with no sealer added, allowing adequate drying time between each application.

3. Slightly dampen the surface with water using the bristle bright. Load the flat with Antique White, then lightly blend on the right side of the dog. Use Black Plum on the left side.

4. Measure and mark a ¹/4" border along all sides. Apply painter's tape along the border for a clean edge, then base using the No. 4 filbert with Lamp Black. When dry, remove the tape. Apply a ¹/8" pinstripe along the border using the liner with Evergreen. Let dry.

5. Trace the pattern from page 74, and transfer the main pattern lines for the dog onto the sign. Transfer details as needed.

Paint

Note: When painting the hair, refer to Tips & Techniques on page 10.

EARS

1. Use the No. 10 chisel blender to apply the background colors. Begin by chiseling with Black Plum, then with Antique White, and finally with Cocoa (**Fig. 1**).

2. Use the filbert grainer to rake the fur with Dark Chocolate. Add darker hairs with Driftwood and Soft Black. Take your time and allow the strokes to follow the direction of the hair growth, varying the width and length for a natural look (**Fig. 2**).

3. Float and chisel the overlapping areas using the No. 10 chisel blender with Lamp Black. Pull short hairs on the top and outside edges of the ears using the liner with Dark Chocolate, again varying the lengths for a natural look. Pull additional hairs with Soft Black (**Fig. 3**).

EYES

1. Use the No. 3 round to base the irises with Cocoa. Shade the outside edges using the No. 6 chisel blender and Milk Chocolate. Use the short liner to line the sides with Soft Black (**Fig. 1**).

2. Base the pupils using the No. 1 round with a wash of Dark Chocolate. Repeat with a Soft Black wash, covering a smaller area. Apply the centers with Lamp Black. Add a Burnt Orange tint to the left and right sides of each pupil (**Fig. 2**).

3. Highlight the irises using the short liner with a brush mix of Cocoa + Snow White. Add sparkle highlights to each pupil with Snow White. Line the eyes with Soft Black, then deepen the tops with Lamp Black. Highlight the bottom of the right eye with Light Buttermilk (**Fig. 3**).

FUR AROUND EYES, MUZZLE, AND TOP OF HEAD

1. Use the No. 6 chisel blender to float and chisel the hair with Dark Chocolate (**Fig. 1**), then deepen with Soft Black. Allow these colors to fade from the top of the head into the snout area (**Fig. 2**).

2. Use the No. 6 chisel blender to float and chisel the hair on the right cheekbone area with Milk Chocolate. Apply Antique White under the eyes and above the right eye. Use Driftwood and Charcoal Grey above the right eye (**Fig. 2**). Deepen the hairs with a touch of Lamp Black (**Fig. 3**).

3. Use a wet-on-wet technique to paint the eyelids. Begin on the inside edge using the No. 1 round with Cocoa, then with Dark Chocolate, and finally with Lamp Black. Use the short liner with Snow White to highlight above and below each eye (**Fig. 3**).

NOSE

1. Use a wet-on-wet technique and the No. 3 round to base the nose. Begin with Dark Chocolate, then apply Soft Black down the middle and for the nostrils (**Fig. 1**).

2. Use the short liner with Light Buttermilk to highlight the middle of the nose and the nostrils. Tint the top middle area of the nose using the No. 6 chisel blender with Charcoal Grey, keeping this color toward the back. Tint the top right corner with Shading Flesh (**Fig. 2**).

3. Deepen the Soft Black shaded areas using the No. 6 chisel blender with a touch of Lamp Black. Highlight the top left of the nose with Light Buttermilk, then brighten with Snow White. Lightly float and chisel Shading Flesh along the top outside edge of the nose. Lightly shade around the outside edge with Soft Black, then deepen with Lamp Black (**Fig. 3**).

MOUTH

1. Loosely base the mouth using the No. 4 filbert with a brush mix of Gooseberry Pink + Snow White. Shade the top of the tongue with Gooseberry Pink, then highlight the bottom with Snow White (**Fig. 1**).

2. Deepen the tongue using the No. 6 chisel blender with Black Plum. Use the same color to line the creases on the tongue. Float and chisel Black Plum along the inside edge of the mouth. Touch a small amount of Shading Flesh just under the two canine teeth (**Fig. 2**).

3. Deepen shading using the No. 6 chisel blender with Soft Black. Highlight the middle inside gum with Light Buttermilk (**Fig. 3**).

4. Paint the teeth using the short liner and a wet-on-wet technique. Start with Light Buttermilk, then touch a small amount of Antique White to the inside area of the teeth for a yellow tinge. Touch Snow White to the outside edge (**Fig. 2**).

5. Use the short liner with Black Plum to line between the bottom teeth to help define and separate them. Use the No. 6 chisel blender with Dark Chocolate to shade the bottom of the mouth on both sides where it meets the stick, then deepen with Soft Black. Highlight the middle of the mouth with Snow White (**Fig. 3**).

MUZZLE, CHEST, AND SNOUT

1. Use the No. 6 filbert with Driftwood to loosely basecoat the muzzle and chest area. Soften the color as you work up the snout toward the top of the head. Use the No. 10 chisel blender with Charcoal Grey to apply shading (**Fig. 1**).

2. Use the filbert grainer to rake or chisel the muzzle, chest, and snout with Light Buttermilk, then brighten with Snow White (**Fig. 2**).

3. Add the freckles using the No. 1 round with Dark Chocolate, then deepen some with Soft Black. Use the short liner to pull Soft Black hairs at the top of the head. Tint the chest and the back left side of the body using the No. 10 chisel blender with Evergreen (**Fig. 3**).

STICK

1. Base using the No. 4 filbert with a loose coat of Slate Grey (**Fig. 1**).

2. Use the No. 10 chisel blender to chisel in Antique White, applying more to the middle and ends of the stick. Shade with a brush mix of Slate Grey + Snow White (**Fig. 2**).

3. Deepen the shading with a touch of Lamp Black. Apply Evergreen tints (**Fig. 3**).

LETTERING

Note: Refer to Tips & Techniques on page 10.

1. Use the liner with Evergreen to letter "NEW YORK KENNEL CLUB". Line the outside edge with Lamp Black.

2. Use the short liner with Lamp Black to letter "Breeding Champions Since 1898".

Finish

1. Antique as described in Tips & Techniques on page 10.

2. When dry, spray with Sealer/Finisher. Let dry.

Fig. 1

Fig. 2

Fig. 3

Perkin's Fruit Wholesalers

*A*ntique enamelware is definitely a trip down memory lane. White enamelware was often trimmed in blue, black, or red. Wholesalers were importers of fruits that were not native to North America.

Palette

◆ *DecoArt* Americana Acrylic Paint: Berry Red, Cadmium Orange, Cadmium Yellow, Charcoal Grey, Cocoa, Dark Chocolate, Hauser Light Green, Hauser Medium Green, Heritage Brick, Lamp Black, Lemon Yellow, Light Buttermilk, Marigold, Milk Chocolate, Napa Red, Neutral Grey, Primary Yellow, Snow White, Soft Black, Yellow Ochre

Brushes

◆ *Princeton:* Select Series 1½" bristle bright, Nos. 6 and 10 chisel blender, ⅜" and ⅝" deerfoot, No. 10 filbert, ½" and ¾" flat wash, No. 10/0 liner, ½" lunar mop, No. 1 script liner, No. 10/0 short liner; Umbria Series No. 12 flat

Surface

◆ *Viking Woodcrafts* Wood Lid, No. 164-1048 (9" x 13"), and Wire Basket with Handles, No. 164-1047 (13" x 9" x 5½")

Other Supplies

◆ *Creative Imaginations* Impress-On rub-ons: Antique Accents, No. 28406; *DecoArt* Americana Acrylic Sealer/Finisher, Matte (spray); *DecoArt* Americana Multi-Purpose Sealer

Prep

1. Lightly sand the lid and wipe to remove dust.

2. Basecoat the lid using the sponge roller with Multi-Purpose Sealer + Light Buttermilk (2:1). When dry, lightly sand and wipe to remove dust. Rebase with two coats of Light Buttermilk with no sealer added, allowing adequate drying time between applications.

3. Trace the pattern from page 75, and transfer the main pattern lines onto the lid. Transfer details as needed.

Paint

Note: Refer to the pattern for placement of shading and highlights.

BACKGROUND

1. Use painter's tape to mask each section of the background as you work to maintain clean edges. Begin with the middle area floor. Use the bristle bright to slightly dampen the surface with water, then use the 5/8" deerfoot to stipple the middle area with Neutral Grey. Use the lunar mop to soften. When dry, redampen the surface and then stipple with Charcoal Grey, covering a narrower area. Mop to soften. Remove the tape. Use the same technique to apply the top section, allowing more of the Light Buttermilk background to show through. Use the same technique for the bottom section; note that this area is the darkest.

2. Slightly dampen the area by the base of the bowl and the bottom of the pear with water. Use the No. 12 flat with Lamp Black to apply shadows. Mop to soften.

BOWL

1. Use the filbert with Light Buttermilk to touch up the bowl, if necessary. Use the No. 12 flat with Neutral Grey to float shading on the sides of the bowl. Mop to soften. Use the No. 10 chisel blender with Neutral Grey to shade under the top rim and along the bottom of the bowl (**Fig. 1**).

2. Intensify the shaded areas with a touch of Lamp Black, using the 3/4" flat wash for the sides of the bowl and the No. 10 chisel blender for the bottom of the bowl. Use the No. 10 chisel blender with Snow White to apply a loose flip-float highlight on the bowl. Mop to soften (**Fig. 2**).

3. Apply the rim with the script liner and Lamp Black. Use the liner to skip Light Buttermilk highlights on the rim, then brighten with Snow White. Apply the chipped areas of the bowl using the same brush with Lamp Black (**Fig. 2**).

4. Use the No. 6 chisel blender to loosely float Milk Chocolate around the chipped areas to create the appearance of rust. Brighten with a touch of Cadmium Orange. Tint the left side of the bowl using the No. 10 chisel blender with Napa Red. Tint the right side of the bowl near the pear with Marigold, then brighten with Cadmium Yellow (**Fig. 3**).

BANANAS

1. Use the filbert to base the bananas with a loose coat of Yellow Ochre. Apply a wash of Marigold to brighten (**Fig. 1**).

2. Apply shading using the 1/2" flat wash with Cocoa, then deepen with Milk Chocolate. Add the darkest areas with a touch of Heritage Brick. Highlight with Cadmium Yellow, then brighten with a brush mix of Cadmium Yellow + Snow White (**Fig. 2**).

3. Apply tints using the No. 6 chisel blender with Hauser Light Green. Add random tints with a wash of Primary Yellow. Apply a wash of Lemon Yellow to the brightest areas. Line the stem with Dark Chocolate. While still wet, shade with Soft Black, then deepen with Lamp Black. Highlight the top of the stem with Snow White. Use the liner with Soft Black to add the ripened spots on the banana, then deepen with Lamp Black, referring to the photo for placement. Float final highlights on the bananas using the No. 10 chisel blender with Snow White (**Fig. 3**).

APPLES

1. Use the filbert to base the apples with a loose coat of Cadmium Yellow. Use the No. 6 chisel blender to loosely float Snow White highlights. Load the side of the same brush with Cadmium Orange and then use the chisel edge to apply streaks (**Fig. 1**).

2. With the No. 10 chisel blender, float and chisel Berry Red, working from the top down and the bottom up. Also float and chisel along the back, pulling in at the stem indentation. Use the No. 6 chisel blender to apply Hauser Medium Green in the stem indentation. With the dirty brush, deepen with Lamp Black. Accent the top right side of the apple with a touch of Hauser Medium Green (**Fig. 2**).

3. Shade the apples using the 3/4" flat wash with Napa Red, then deepen with Napa Red + a touch of Lamp Black. The darkest shadows are on the small apple where it meets the large apple. This will help to "push" the small apple behind the large apple. Use the liner with Dark Chocolate to line the stem. Skip Lamp Black on the right side of the stem and Snow White on the left side. Use the short liner with Snow White to add sparkle highlights to the large apple (**Fig 3**).

PEAR

1. Use the filbert to base the pear with a loose coat of Cadmium Yellow. Slightly dampen the pear with water, then stipple highlights with the 3/8" deerfoot and Lemon Yellow. Mop to soften. When dry, repeat to brighten using Snow White, this time covering a smaller area (**Fig. 1**).

2. Use the 1/2" flat wash to shade Marigold around the outside edges of the pear, pulling in toward the center. Use the No. 6 chisel blender to shade inside the stem area with Marigold. Deepen the shading with Milk Chocolate, then intensify the darkest areas with a touch of Dark Chocolate (**Fig. 2**).

3. Add tints using the No. 10 chisel blender with Heritage Brick and Hauser Light Green. Line the stem with Dark Chocolate. Shade the bottom of the stem with lines of Lamp Black, then highlight the top with Snow White (**Fig. 3**).

FINAL SHADING

1. Use the 1/2" flat wash with Lamp Black to deepen the shading on the left side of the bowl.

2. Use the No. 6 chisel blender with Lamp Black to deepen the shadows under the bowl and pear and on the bowl above the pear.

3. Lightly shade the top corners of the lid with Lamp Black.

LETTERING

Note: Refer to Tips & Techniques on page 10.

1. Use the liner with Lamp Black to letter "PERKIN'S FRUIT WHOLESALERS". Highlight the left side of each letter with Cadmium Yellow.

2. Use the short liner with Berry Red to letter "Freshness Guaranteed".

3. Use the short liner with Light Buttermilk to letter "Hand Packed Since 1901".

Finish

1. Apply a desired Antique Accents rub-on to each corner of the lid.

2. When dry, spray with Sealer/Finisher. Let dry.

Fig. 1

Fig. 2

Fig. 3

Alley Cat Licorice Co.

*T*his slogan really brings to mind the days when a penny was frequently used to make purchases. It's hard to imagine today that you could once purchase ten pieces of candy for one cent!

Palette

◆ *DecoArt* Americana Acrylic Paint: Antique White, Burnt Sienna, Cadmium Yellow, Charcoal Grey, Cocoa, Colonial Green, Flesh Tone, Hauser Light Green, Khaki Tan, Lamp Black, Light Buttermilk, Milk Chocolate, Navy Blue, Neutral Grey, Payne's Grey, Shading Flesh, Snow White, Soft Black, Tangerine

Brushes

◆ *Princeton:* Select Series Nos. 8 and 10 chisel blender, No. 2 filbert, ⅛" and ¼" filbert grainer, No. 10/0 liner, No. 1 round, No. 10/0 script liner, No. 10/0 short liner

Surface

◆ *Simply Cotton* Tin Sign (12½" x 9½")

Other Supplies

◆ *DecoArt* Americana Acrylic Sealer/Finisher, Matte (spray); *DecoArt* Americana Multi-Purpose Sealer

Prep

1. Wipe the tin sign with a mix of water and vinegar (1:1). Rinse with clear water, then let dry. Create a Dark Grey Mix with Lamp Black + Charcoal Grey (1:1). Basecoat the tin sign using the sponge roller with Multi-Purpose Sealer + Dark Grey Mix (2:1). When dry, lightly sand and wipe to remove dust. Rebase with two coats of the Dark Grey Mix with no sealer added, allowing adequate drying time between applications.

2. Measure and mark a 1/4" border along all sides. Apply painter's tape along the inside of the border for a clean edge, then base using the No. 1 round with Burnt Sienna. When dry, remove tape. Apply a 1/8" pinstripe along the border using the round with Light Buttermilk. Let dry.

3. Trace the pattern from page 76, and transfer the main pattern lines for the cat and lettering onto the sign. Transfer details as needed.

Paint

Note: Refer to the pattern for placement of shading and highlights. When painting the fur, refer to Tips & Technique on page 10.

FUR

1. Use the 1/4" filbert grainer with Khaki Tan to rake the first layer of fur, allowing some of the background color to show through for the dark markings. Take your time and allow the strokes to follow the direction of the fur growth, making sure to vary the lengths for a natural look (**Fig. 1**).

2. Use the No. 8 chisel blender to apply Cocoa and Milk Chocolate tints; this will help to warm up the cat's coat. For color variation and filler, use the 1/8" filbert grainer to rake more fur with Neutral Grey.

3. Rake the lighter fur with Antique White (**Fig. 2**). Brighten first with Light Buttermilk and then with Snow White (**Fig. 3**).

4. Use the No. 8 chisel blender to chisel Payne's Grey through the dark areas, then repeat with a touch of Lamp Black (**Fig. 3**).

5. To avoid creating solid-looking stripes, use the short liner to pull Neutral Grey hairs at the top of the head and Antique White hairs on the chest area (**Fig. 3**).

NOSE

Note: The nose is painted using a wet-on-wet technique.

1. Base the nose with the No. 1 round and Shading Flesh (**Fig. 1**).

2. While still wet, pick up a touch of Burnt Sienna, wipe on a paper towel to remove excess paint, then add the dark areas around the outside edge of the nose, lightly blending this into the basecoat color. If this area becomes too dark, lighten the middle with a touch of Shading Flesh (**Fig. 2**).

3. Use the short liner with Light Buttermilk to highlight the middle of the nose. Line the outside

edge of the nose with Lamp Black. Use the No. 8 chisel blender with Lamp Black to shade the right side of the nose. Shade around the left and right sides with Soft Black. Tint the cheeks with the No. 8 chisel blender and Shading Flesh (**Fig. 3**).

RIGHT EAR

1. Use the filbert and a wet-on-wet technique to paint the right ear. Begin with Flesh Tone, then while still wet, stroke the light areas with Light Buttermilk (**Fig. 2**).

2. Apply Khaki Tan and then deepen with Soft Black. Use the liner to apply the outside edge with Khaki Tan (**Fig. 3**).

LEFT EAR

1. Use the 1/8" filbert grainer with Neutral Grey to rake the tufts of hair emerging from inside the left ear flap (**Fig. 1**).

2. Rake the lighter hairs with Antique White and Light Buttermilk. Use the No. 10 chisel blender with Khaki Tan to shade around the outside edge of the inner ear (**Fig. 2**).

3. Line the outside edge of the ear using the liner with Khaki Tan, then accent with Light Buttermilk. Add tints to the middle of the inner area of the ear using the No. 8 chisel blender with Shading Flesh. Use the No. 10 chisel blender with Soft Black to shade the right side and along the bottom of the ear (**Fig. 3**).

EYES

1. Use the short liner with Snow White to place a thin line around the pupils and irises. Use the same color to line the veins in the irises (**Fig. 1**).

2. Place Hauser Light Green and Colonial Green between the veins. Overcoat the white veins with Burnt Sienna. Line the outside edge of the pupil with Tangerine, then add the tiny lines with Burnt Sienna (**Fig. 2**).

3. Use the No. 8 chisel blender to shade the outside edge of each eye with a brush mix of Navy Blue + Snow White. Use the same brush with

Cadmium Yellow to apply tints to both sides of the eyes. Shade the tops with Payne's Grey. Use the short liner to add highlight sparkles of Light Buttermilk. Use the same brush to line Lamp Black beneath the eyes (**Fig. 3**).

FRECKLES AND WHISKERS

1. Apply the freckles using the tip of the short liner with Payne's Grey.

2. Use the script liner with Light Buttermilk to pull the whiskers.

LETTERING

Note: Refer to Tips & Techniques on page 10.

1. Use the liner with Light Buttermilk to letter "ALLEY CAT LICORICE CO."

2. Use the short liner with Light Buttermilk to letter "World's Finest" and "Ten For A Penny".

Finish

When dry, spray with Sealer/Finisher. Let dry.

Fig. 1

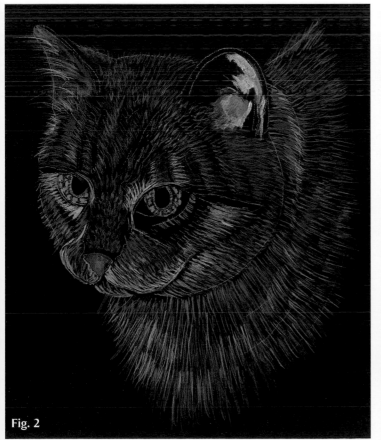
Fig. 2

Fig. 3

Stony Creek Blacksmiths

A blacksmith is a person who creates objects from iron or steel by forging metal. The original fuel for forge fires was coal. Horse owners required the service of a blacksmith to have shoes sized and fitted to their horses.

Palette

◆ *DecoArt* Americana Acrylic Paint: Antique White, Charcoal Grey, Dark Chocolate, Driftwood, Lamp Black, Light Buttermilk, Light Cinnamon, Neutral Grey, Payne's Grey, Snow White, Soft Black, Terra Cotta, Traditional Burnt Sienna

Brushes

◆ *Princeton*: Select Series 1½" bristle bright, Nos. 8 and 10 chisel blender, ⅝" deerfoot, No. 10/0 liner, ½" lunar mop, No. 3 round, No. 10/0 short liner; Umbria Series No. 12 flat

Surface

◆ *Coyote Woodworks* MDF Large Ginger Bread Plaque, No. P102 (14½" x 11¾")

Other Supplies

◆ *DecoArt* Americana DuraClear Matte Varnish; *DecoArt* Americana Multi-Purpose Sealer

Prep

1. Lightly sand the plaque and wipe to remove dust.

2. Basecoat the plaque using the sponge roller with Multi-Purpose Sealer + Light Buttermilk (2:1). When dry, lightly sand and wipe to remove dust. Use the No. 3 round with Lamp Black + Multi-Purpose Sealer (2:1) to base the routed areas. Use the flat side of the sponge roller with the same mix to basecoat the sides of the plaque. Rebase the plaque, excluding the routed areas, using Light Buttermilk with no sealer added. Base the routed areas and sides of plaque using Lamp Black with no sealer added. Let dry.

3. Use the No. 12 flat to shade Neutral Grey around the outside edge of the plaque. Use the lunar mop to soften. Slightly dampen the surface with water using the bristle bright, then use the deerfoot to softly stipple Neutral Grey to widen the shading. Mop to soften. Let dry. Dampen the surface with water, then use the deerfoot with Charcoal Grey to stipple around the edge to intensify the shading in a narrower area. Mop to soften. Use the flat to apply a hint of Lamp Black shading around the outside edge. Mop to soften.

4. Trace the pattern from page 77, and transfer the main pattern lines onto the plaque, carefully maintaining the angular bone structure of the legs. Transfer details as needed.

Paint

Note: Refer to the pattern for placement of shading and highlights.

BASECOAT

1. Use the No. 3 round to basecoat the horse with one rough coat of Light Cinnamon. Do not base the blaze on the face, as this will remain the Light Buttermilk background color (**Fig. 1**).

2. Base the hooves with Driftwood (**Fig. 1**).

COAT

Note: Create the muscles of the face, neck, body, and legs by skimming the surface with shades and highlights as indicated on the pattern and on the step-by-step worksheets and by stroking in the direction of the hairs as they flow over the muscles. Use the short liner for the smaller areas of the face, the No. 10 chisel blender for the larger muscles of the body, and the No. 8 chisel blender for the legs.

1. Use the No. 12 flat to apply the large shaded areas on the underbelly and on the neck and chest area beneath the head. Begin the shaded areas with Dark Chocolate (**Fig. 1**), then deepen with Soft Black (**Fig. 2**). Accent the deepest shadows with a touch of Lamp Black. Mop to soften (**Fig. 3**).

2. Once the shaded areas have been established, use the No. 8 chisel blender to build highlights first with Terra Cotta, then with Antique White, and finally with Light Buttermilk (**Fig. 3**). Each lighter color should cover a smaller area than the previous color.

MANE

1. Use the short liner to sparingly base the mane with strokes of Light Cinnamon (**Fig. 1**). Add strokes of Traditional Burnt Sienna and Terra Cotta (**Fig. 2**). Keep the strokes loose, using slightly different lengths and curvatures for a natural look. Accent the mane at the neck and on the forehead with Soft Black strokes (**Fig. 3**).

MOUTH AND NOSTRILS

1. Base the mouth using the No. 3 round with Payne's Grey, being careful to maintain the angular shape of the muzzle (**Fig. 2**).

2. Base the nostrils using the No. 3 round with Charcoal Grey. Accent the deepest nostril shadows with Lamp Black. Use short liner to highlight the flared shapes with Light Buttermilk (**Fig. 3**).

BLAZE

1. Loosely apply Light Buttermilk down the center of the face with the No. 3 round, allowing the edges of the shape to be somewhat irregular and jagged (**Fig. 3**).

Fig. 1

EYES

1. Base the eyes and extend the eye-lashes using the short liner with Lamp Black (**Fig. 2**).

2. Use the same brush with Light Buttermilk to add reflections and highlights (**Fig. 3**).

TAIL

1. Use the liner to apply the tail first with a few sparse strokes of Light Cinnamon (**Fig. 2**) and then with additional strokes of Dark Chocolate (**Fig. 2**). Keep the strokes loose and flowing, using varying pressure to create different stroke widths. For a more natural tail, use different lengths and stroke curvatures; allow some strokes to naturally cross over others. Complete the tail with accent strokes of brush-mixed Charcoal Grey + Light Buttermilk (**Fig. 3**).

HOOVES

1. Use the No. 8 chisel blender to shade the hooves with vertical strokes of Charcoal Grey, then deepen with Lamp Black (**Fig. 2**).

2. Highlight each hoof with vertical strokes of Snow White (**Fig. 3**).

LETTERING

Note: Refer to Tips & Techniques on page 10.

Use the liner with Traditional Burnt Sienna to letter "STONY CREEK BLACKSMITHS".

Finish

When dry, spray with Sealer/Finisher. Let dry.

Fig. 2

Fig. 3

Clancy's Automotive Service & Repair

Can you believe that when it was new, this 1955 Second Series Chevy 3100 stepside would have cost $2,207? This truck was originally used on a wheat farm in Kansas from 1955 until 2003, and now "resides" in Cadmus, Ontario. The original color of the truck was Ocean Green. Truly a classic!

Palette

◆ *DecoArt* Americana Acrylic Paint: Black Green, Black Plum, Burnt Orange, Cadmium Yellow, Charcoal Grey, Dark Chocolate, Driftwood, Flesh Tone, Hauser Dark Green, Hauser Light Green, Hauser Medium Green, Heritage Brick, Khaki Tan, Lamp Black, Light Buttermilk, Milk Chocolate, Moon Yellow, Payne's Grey, Sea Breeze, Slate Grey, Snow White, Soft Black, Tuscan Red
◆ *DecoArt* Americana Neons: Fiery Red

Brushes

◆ *Princeton:* Select Series 1½" bristle bright, Nos. 6 and 10 chisel blender, No. 8 filbert, No. 10/0 liner, ¼" and 1" lunar blender, ½" lunar mop, Nos. 2 and 3 round, No. 18/0 short liner; Synthetic Sable Series 1½" flat wash

Surface

◆ *Coyote Woodworks* MDF Lattice Tray with Insert, No. T100 (15¼" x 11¼" x 4")

Other Supplies

◆ *DecoArt* Americana Acrylic Sealer/Finisher, Matte (spray); *DecoArt* Americana Multi-Purpose Sealer

Prep

1. Lightly sand the tray and insert and wipe to remove dust.

2. Basecoat the insert using the sponge roller with Multi-Purpose Sealer + Khaki Tan (2:1). When dry, lightly sand and wipe to remove dust. Rebase with two coats of Khaki Tan with no sealer added, allowing adequate drying time between applications.

3. Basecoat the tray using the bristle bright with Multi-Purpose Sealer + Lamp Black (2:1). When dry, lightly sand and wipe to remove dust. Rebase with two coats of Lamp Black with no sealer added, allowing adequate drying time between applications.

4. Measure and mark a 1/4" border along all sides of the insert. Apply painter's tape along the border for a clean edge, then base using the filbert with Lamp Black. When dry, remove tape. Apply a 1/8" pinstripe along the border using the No. 2 round with Heritage Brick. Let dry.

5. Trace the pattern from page 78, and transfer the main pattern lines onto the insert. Transfer details as needed.

Paint

GROUND AREA

Note: The ground area directly beneath the truck is fairly dark and gradually lightens as you work away from it.

1. Use painter's tape to mask the area above the ground for a clean edge. Use the 1 1/2" flat wash with Black Green to apply the grass area beneath the truck. Use the lunar mop to soften. Let dry. Repeat as needed until you achieve adequate coverage.

2. Using the 1" lunar blender, drybrush with Lamp Black to deepen the shading. Pick up Hauser Medium Green on the dirty brush and softly blend onto the ground area, placing more in front of the front left tire.

Fig. 1

3. Use the No. 3 round to wash a Lamp Black shadow under the truck. Use the lunar mop to soften.

TRUCK BASECOATS

Note: This truck is painted to appear old and weathered. Refer to the step-by-step color worksheets for color placement. These colors can overlap a bit in areas or be deepened or lightened a little more here and there. For example, Charcoal Grey can be deepened in some areas with Lamp Black and Tuscan Red can be brightened in some areas with Fiery Red. Some of the colors can be floated, but to achieve a distressed finish, it is best to use a drybrush technique with the 1/4" lunar blender. When drybrushing, follow the contour of the truck.

1. Basecoat the truck using the filbert with Heritage Brick. Apply the linework using the liner with Lamp Black. Basecoat the wheel wells using the No. 2 round with Soft Black (**Fig. 1**). Wash the rim above the window with thinned Lamp Black (**Fig. 2**).

2. Use the 1/4" lunar blender to distress the truck first with Flesh Tone and then with touches of Hauser Medium Green and Moon Yellow (**Fig. 2**). Add darker areas using Charcoal Grey with random touches of Lamp Black. Apply brighter areas with Tuscan Red, then brighten here and there with Fiery Red (**Fig. 3**).

3. Use the short liner with Lamp Black to line the grille just under the windshield (**Fig. 2**). Apply the vertical lines with Tuscan Red (**Fig. 3**).

DOOR

1. Wash the sign area using the filbert with Tuscan Red (**Fig. 1**). To distress, use the 1/4" lunar blender to drybrush with Dark Chocolate, Hauser Medium Green, and a touch of Burnt Orange (**Fig. 2**). Age further by using the short liner to skim the door with long and short lines of thinned Slate Grey and thinned Light Buttermilk (**Fig. 3**).

2. Use short liner to line the handle with Slate Grey (**Fig. 1**). Skip Lamp Black along the bottom (**Fig. 2**) and Light Buttermilk along the top (**Fig. 3**).

Fig. 2

TRUCK INTERIOR
1. Base the interior of the truck using the No. 3 round with Soft Black (**Fig. 1**).

2. Use the No. 10 chisel blender to shade Lamp Black along the top and by the driver's door. Float the seat on the driver's side with Black Plum, then brighten with Tuscan Red. Use the short liner with a mix of Black Plum + Snow White to detail the seat and around the passenger-side window. Use the same mix to float and chisel highlights along the top of the seat. Use the short liner to line the steering wheel with Black Plum. Skip Lamp Black along the bottom and Light Buttermilk along the top. Line the inside edge of the window with Lamp Black (**Fig. 2**).

3. Use the No. 10 chisel blender to create the windows with a wash of Light Buttermilk. Accent the outside edge of the front passenger-side window with Snow White. Use the same color with the No. 6 chisel blender to create the glass glare. Tint the passenger-side window with Sea Breeze.

GRILLE AND ACCESSORIES
1. Base the front grille area using the No. 3 round with a loose coat of Soft Black (**Fig. 1**). Use the No. 2 round with Driftwood to apply the bars. Shade with the No. 6 chisel blender and Charcoal Grey. Use the No. 2 round to skim Light Buttermilk highlights on the vertical bars and the No. 6 chisel blender to chisel highlights on the horizontal bars (**Fig. 2**). Use the 1/4" lunar blender to distress the grille with Dark Chocolate and Burnt Orange (**Fig. 3**).

2. Base the hood emblem, mirror, gas cap, and molding on the side of the truck using the No. 2 round with Slate Grey (**Fig. 1**). Use the No. 6 chisel blender to shade with Charcoal Grey, then deepen with Lamp Black (**Fig. 2**). Highlight with Light Buttermilk, then brighten with Snow White (**Fig. 3**).

3. Use the liner with Slate Grey to line the windshield wipers. Skip Lamp Black along the bottoms and Snow White along the tops.

HEADLIGHTS AND TURN SIGNAL LIGHTS
1. Base the lights using the No. 2 round with Slate Grey (**Fig. 1**), then shade with Charcoal Grey.

2. Add details using the short liner with Lamp Black (**Fig. 2**). Highlight with Light Buttermilk, then add brighter highlights with Snow White (**Fig. 3**).

CORN
1. Tape off the top edge of the truck to keep it clean. Use the No. 2 round to base the corn with Moon Yellow. Use the No. 6 chisel blender with Milk Chocolate to apply shading (**Fig. 1**).

2. Use the short liner with Cadmium Yellow to create the kernels. Line the husks using the liner with Hauser Medium Green, Hauser Dark Green, and Black Green. Highlight with Hauser Light Green (**Fig. 2**).

3. Use the No. 6 chisel blender with Lamp Black to separate the husks. Add final highlights with a brush mix of Hauser Light Green + Snow White (**Fig. 3**).

TIRES
1. Base the tires using the No. 3 round and Payne's Grey. Line the whitewalls with Light Buttermilk. Base the rims with Heritage Brick and the hubcaps with Slate Grey (**Fig. 1**).

2. Drybrush treads on the front tire using the 1/4" lunar blender with Slate Grey. Distress the rims with Flesh Tone, Tuscan Red, and Lamp Black (**Fig. 2**).

3. Use the No. 6 chisel blender to shade the hubcap with Charcoal Grey, then deepen with Lamp Black. Highlight with Light Buttermilk, then brighten with Snow White. Skip Dark Chocolate along the whitewalls (**Fig. 3**).

BUMPERS
1. Base the front bumper using the No. 3 round with Light Buttermilk (**Fig. 1**). Use the No. 10 chisel blender to float and chisel shading with Charcoal Grey (**Fig. 2**). Shade along the top with Dark Chocolate. Line the bolts with Charcoal Grey. Highlight the top of the bolts with Snow White (**Fig. 3**).

2. Base the rear bumper using the No. 2 round with Slate Grey (**Fig. 1**). Use the No. 6 chisel blender with Charcoal Grey to shade (**Fig. 2**), then distress using the 1/4" lunar blender with Dark Chocolate (**Fig. 3**).

STEP RAIL

1. Base using the No. 2 round with a loose coat of Heritage Brick (**Fig. 1**).

2. Use the short liner to add lines through the middle with Dark Chocolate. While still wet, streak with Light Buttermilk (**Fig. 2**). When dry, apply a few lines with Lamp Black. Line the bottom edge with Flesh Tone (**Fig. 3**).

LETTERING

Note: Refer to Tips & Techniques on page 10.

1. Use the liner with Heritage Brick to letter

"Clancy's". Skip Fiery Red through the middle of these letters.

2. Use the short liner with Lamp Black to letter "AUTOMOTIVE SERVICE & REPAIR" and "We Can Fix Anything!"

3. Use the short liner with Light Buttermilk to letter "Windy Ridge Farm" on the driver's door.

𝓕𝓲𝓷𝓲𝓼𝓱

1. Antique as described in Tips & Techniques on page 10.

2. When dry, spray with Sealer/Finisher. Let dry.

3. Place the insert into the tray.

Fig. 3

New England Tin Works

*S*killed artisans known as tinsmiths began actively plying their trade in America in the early eighteenth century. Using a few basic tools, they made a variety of containers, expensive show boxes, and tin liners for ice boxes.

Palette

◆ *DecoArt* Americana Acrylic Paint: Black Green, Burnt Orange, Cadmium Yellow, Citron Green, Dark Chocolate, Hauser Dark Green, Hauser Light Green, Hauser Medium Green, Heritage Brick, Honey Brown, Lamp Black, Light Buttermilk, Marigold, Milk Chocolate, Moon Yellow, Soft Black, Snow White, Traditional Burnt Sienna, Tuscan Red
◆ *DecoArt* Americana Neons: Fiery Red

Brushes

◆ *Princeton:* Select Series 1½" bristle bright, Nos. 8 and 12 chisel blender, ¼" and ⅜" deerfoot, No. 10 filbert, 1" lunar blender, ½" lunar mop, No. 0 round, No. 10/0 short liner; Umbria Series No. 12 flat

Surface

◆ 9" x 12" stretched canvas

Other Supplies

◆ *Creative Imaginations* Impress-On rub-ons: Antique Accents No. 28406, and Sepia No. 28405; *DecoArt* Americana Acrylic Sealer/Finisher, Matte (spray)

Prep

1. Basecoat the canvas using the sponge roller with Heritage Brick. When dry, apply a second coat. Let dry.

2. Trace the pattern from page 80, and transfer the main pattern lines onto the canvas. Transfer details as needed.

3. Create an aged appearance by drybrushing the canvas with Lamp Black. Drag the lunar blender vertically along the top and bottom of the canvas, along the sides of the canvas, and to the left of the tin container.

4. Embellish the corners and sides of the canvas with the desired Antique Accents rub-ons, referring to the photo for placement.

5. Use the lunar blender to lightly drybrush Lamp Black over the rub-ons to help blend them into the background.

6. Drybrush Tuscan Red to brighten some areas on the canvas, particularly to the right of the tin container. Brighten further with a touch of Fiery Red.

Paint

Note: Refer to the pattern for placement of shading and highlights.

TIN

1. Base the tin container using the filbert with Moon Yellow and let dry. Use the bristle bright with water to slightly dampen the tin, then use the 3/8" deerfoot to stipple Milk Chocolate shading, placing it mostly along the outside edges. Use the lunar mop to soften. Let dry. Repeat this technique with Traditional Burnt Sienna, using less paint and covering a narrower area. Mop to soften (**Fig. 1**). Let dry.

2. Use the No. 12 chisel blender to float and chisel Dark Chocolate randomly around the top and outside edges of the tin (**Fig. 2**), then deepen with Soft Black. Use the 3/8" deerfoot to apply

Cadmium Yellow highlights in the middle of the tin. Let dry.

3. Apply the Sepia rub-ons of choice to the tin, referring to the photo for placement. Slightly age by drybrushing as in Prep step 5, if desired.

SUNFLOWER PETALS

1. Paint one petal at a time using the round and working wet-on-wet. Begin with the darkest value of Honey Brown, placing more at the base of each petal and where one petal lays behind another. While still wet, base the remaining area of each petal with Marigold. While still wet, apply Moon Yellow highlights in the brighter areas, placing more at the tips and where one petal lays on top of another (**Fig. 1**).

2. When the petals are completed, use the No. 8 or No. 12 chisel blender, depending on the size of the petal, to float and chisel a small amount of Burnt Orange + a touch of Heritage Brick near the base of each petal (**Fig. 2**).

Fig. 1

3. Highlight the tips of the petals, especially the large middle flower, using the No. 8 chisel blender with Cadmium Yellow, then brighten with Snow White (**Fig. 3**).

LEAVES

1. Base the leaves using the filbert with Hauser Medium Green (**Fig. 1**).

2. Float and chisel the shading using the No. 12 chisel blender with Hauser Dark Green, then deepen with Black Green (**Fig. 2**).

3. Use the same brush to add highlights with Hauser Light Green, then brighten with Citron Green. Apply the brightest highlights with Snow White (**Fig. 3**).

SUNFLOWER CENTERS

1. Use the 1/4" deerfoot with Milk Chocolate to stipple the flower centers (**Fig. 1**).

2. Deepen the centers and outside edges with Soft Black (**Fig. 2**).

3. Use the short liner to pull short hairs of Lamp Black in the darker areas and Honey Brown in the lighter areas. Highlight with lines of Light Buttermilk (**Fig. 3**).

LETTERING

Note: Refer to Tips & Techniques on page 10.

1. Use the short liner with Tuscan Red to letter "NEW ENGLAND". Line the right side of each letter with Lamp Black.

2. Use the same brush with Lamp Black to apply the lettering and date for "TIN WORKS Est. 1860".

Finish

When dry, spray with Sealer/Finisher. Let dry.

Fig. 2

Fig. 3

Webster's Towing

*T*he first tow trucks were made in 1915 and were referred to as the "hook and chain." The roads back then were a little rough and bumpy, and drivers were generally inexperienced. Tow trucks not only brought disabled cars into shops, but also helped to prevent drivers and mechanics from working on the roadside in the dark or in bad weather. This tow truck is more than a little worn out—its flat tire can attest to years of use.

Palette

◆ *DecoArt* Americana Acrylic Paint: Bahama Blue, Black Green, Burnt Orange, Butter, Dark Chocolate, Desert Turquoise, Hauser Dark Green, Hauser Medium Green, Heritage Brick, Honey Brown, Lamp Black, Light Buttermilk, Navy Blue, Neutral Grey, Payne's Grey, Snow White, Soft Black, Traditional Burnt Sienna, Turquoise Blue, White Wash
◆ *DecoArt* Americana Neons: Fiery Red

Brushes

◆ *Princeton:* Select Series Nos. 4, 6, 8, and 12 chisel blender; ⅛" and ¼" deerfoot; No. 10/0 liner; ⅛" and 1" lunar blender; ½" lunar mop; No. 3 round; No. 18/0 short liner; Synthetic Sable Series 1½" flat wash

Surface

◆ *Coyote Woodworks* MDF Lattice Tray with Insert, No. T100 (15¼" x 11¼" x 4")

Other Supplies

◆ *DecoArt* Americana Acrylic Sealer/Finisher, Matte (spray); *DecoArt* Americana Multi-Purpose Sealer; *Winsor & Newton* Winton Oil Colour: Raw Umber; odorless thinner

Prep

1. Lightly sand the tray and insert and wipe to remove dust.

2. Basecoat the insert using the sponge roller with Multi-Purpose Sealer + White Wash (2:1). When dry, lightly sand and wipe to remove dust. Rebase with two coats of White Wash with no sealer added, allowing adequate drying time between applications.

3. Basecoat the tray using the bristle bright with Multi-Purpose Sealer + Lamp Black (2:1). When dry, lightly sand and wipe to remove dust. Rebase with two coats of Lamp Black with no sealer added, allowing adequate drying time between applications.

4. Measure and mark a 1/4" border along all sides of the insert. Apply painter's tape along the border for a clean edge, then base with Lamp Black. When dry, remove tape. Apply a 1/8" pinstripe along the border using the round with Heritage Brick. Let dry.

5. Trace the pattern from page 79, and transfer the main pattern lines onto the insert. Transfer details as needed.

Paint

Note: Refer to the pattern for placement of shading and highlights.

GROUND AREA

Note: The ground area directly beneath the truck is fairly dark and gradually lightens as you work away from it.

1. Use painter's tape to mask the area above the ground for a clean edge. Use the 1 1/2" flat wash with Hauser Dark Green to apply the grass area beneath the truck. Use the lunar mop to soften. Let dry. Repeat as needed until you achieve adequate coverage.

2. Drybrush Black Green with the 1" lunar blender to extend the shading. Pick up Hauser Medium Green in the dirty brush and softly blend onto the ground area, placing more by the front left tire.

3. Use the No. 12 chisel blender to wash a Lamp Black shadow under the truck. Mop to soften.

TRUCK BASECOATS

Note: Create a Light Blue Mix of Snow White + Bahama Blue (3:1) to be used throughout the following instructions.

1. Basecoat the top part of the truck using the No. 3 round and Butter. Basecoat the bottom of the truck with the Light Blue Mix. Use the No. 3 round with Dark Chocolate to base the truck interior and the side mirror on the outside of the truck (**Fig. 1**).

2. Base the tires using the No. 3 round with Payne's Grey. When painting the outside edge of the front left tire, load the brush with Payne's Grey and pick up a small amount of Snow White. Base the wheel wells and the area under the ajar hood with Payne's Grey. Use the Light Blue Mix for the front hubcap. Base the running boards and rear hubcap with Dark Chocolate. Base the hoist at the rear of the truck with Heritage Brick. The mirror on the hoist is Neutral Grey (**Fig. 1**).

TRUCK INTERIOR

1. Wash the inside of the truck, excluding the rearview mirror, with Lamp Black. Use the short liner with Dark Chocolate to apply the steering wheel. While still wet, skip Lamp Black along the bottom of the steering wheel and Butter along the top (**Fig. 1**).

2. Float and chisel the inside of the roof using the No. 8 chisel blender with Lamp Black (**Fig. 2**).

WINDOWS

1. Softly wash in the windows using the No. 12 chisel blender with Light Buttermilk. This may take a couple of washes and may be applied in a streaky manner.

2. When dry, use the No. 6 chisel blender to apply a touch of the Light Blue Mix on the windows and against both bottom sides of the center pillar. Line around the edge of the windows with Lamp Black (**Fig. 3**).

FRONT GRILLE

1. Use the No. 6 chisel blender to float and chisel the colors on the front grille, starting with Traditional Burnt Sienna (**Fig. 1**), then with Payne's Grey, and finally with Desert Turquoise (**Fig. 2**).

2. Line details using the liner with Lamp Black.

3. Use the 1/8" deerfoot to stipple with Lamp Black (**Fig. 3**).

PUSH BUMPER

1. The push bumper at the front of the truck is stippled with the 1/4" deerfoot using a wet-on-wet technique. Tape off the outside edge just below the top for clean lines. Stipple the entire area with Honey Brown, then stipple with Dark Chocolate. Blend, then deepen with Soft Black. Blend. Stipple with Traditional Burnt Sienna and brighten here and there with Burnt Orange (**Fig. 2**). Let dry.

2. Lightly stipple Bahama Blue near the top and bottom of the bumper. Use the liner to apply the top edge with Honey Brown. While still wet, skip Lamp Black along the bottom and Traditional Burnt Sienna along the top. When dry, line the highlights with Snow White. Apply the attachment bar at the right using the same technique, but do not highlight (**Fig. 3**).

3. The tow hook is located in the middle of the push bumper. Line the outside edges of the hook using the short liner with Lamp Black. Use the No. 4 chisel blender with Lamp Black to shade under the top of the tow hook (**Fig. 3**).

SIDE-VIEW MIRROR
1. Use the No. 4 chisel blender with Soft Black to shade along the top, bottom, and right side of the side-view mirror. Deepen shading with Lamp Black (**Fig. 1**). Shade the left side with Traditional Burnt Sienna, then highlight with Burnt Orange (**Fig. 2**). Use the 1/8" deerfoot to lightly stipple with Honey Brown (**Fig. 3**).

2. Use the liner with Dark Chocolate to apply the support bracket (**Fig. 1**). Skip Lamp Black along

the bottom and Honey Brown along the top (**Fig. 2**). Add a Light Buttermilk dot for the bolt. Use the liner to skip Light Buttermilk highlights along the top of the bracket (**Fig. 3**).

RUNNING BOARDS
1. Use the short liner with Lamp Black to apply zigzagging linework along the side of the step rail (**Fig. 1**).

2. Use the No. 12 chisel blender to float and chisel Soft Black shading, then deepen with Lamp Black. Float the left side with Heritage Brick, then deepen with Soft Black (**Fig. 2**).

3. Float and chisel the running boards using No. 6 chisel blender with Honey Brown, Traditional Burnt Sienna, and Dark Chocolate (**Fig. 3**)

RUST SPOTS
Note: This truck is painted to appear old and weathered. Use a drybrush technique with the 1/8" lunar blender to apply the rust spots. Drag the brush in one direction, following the contour

Fig. 1

of the truck. Note that there is not much shading and highlighting on the truck. The body sections are defined by the rust areas and moldings. After applying the shape of the rust with the lunar blender, use the No. 6 chisel blender to float and chisel more color, particularly to achieve a clean edge between body sections. Finally, use the 1/8" deerfoot to stipple more rust.

1. The colors for the rust on the blue parts of the truck are Heritage Brick, Bahama Blue (**Fig. 1**), Turquoise Blue, Navy Blue (**Fig. 2**), Dark Chocolate, Soft Black, and Lamp Black. Brighten in between with Snow White (**Fig. 3**). Use the No. 12 chisel blender on the door to apply Bahama Blue and Turquoise Blue. Deepen with a small amount of Navy Blue (**Fig 2**). Brighten the center with Snow White (**Fig. 3**).

2. Add rust areas to the top (light yellow) part of the truck using the 1/8" lunar blender with Traditional Burnt Sienna, then deepen some areas with Dark Chocolate and a touch of Soft Black. Shade the hood and roof using the No. 12 chisel blender with the Light Blue Mix. Separate the body sections and moldings with fine lines of Soft Black (**Fig. 3**).

HEADLIGHTS

1. Base with the No. 3 round and Light Buttermilk (**Fig. 1**). Use the No. 8 chisel blender to shade the tops and bottoms with Neutral Grey, then deepen with Lamp Black (**Fig. 2**).

2. Use the short liner with Snow White to apply highlights, placing them mainly in the center of each light. Line the outside edges with Lamp Black (**Fig. 3**).

BACK HOIST

1. The rear hoist area is kept fairly simple. Paint the rust areas with Neutral Grey + Snow White (1:1) (**Fig. 1**).

2. Use the No. 8 chisel blender with Lamp Black to shade the hoist. Apply the hook using the short liner with Neutral Grey. Line the inside edge of the hook with Lamp Black (**Fig. 2**).

3. Use the 1/8" deerfoot to stipple the brighter red areas on the hoist with Fiery Red. Line the cable with Lamp Black (**Fig. 3**).

Fig. 2

Horn

1. Base the front section using the No. 3 round with Neutral Grey. Base the back section with Dark Chocolate (**Fig. 1**).

2. Use the short liner with Lamp Black to line the edges. Shade the back section using the No. 6 chisel blender with Lamp Black (**Fig. 2**).

3. Highlight the front with Light Buttermilk. Apply a small dot in the center with Dark Chocolate (**Fig. 3**).

Tires

1. Shade the tires, wheel wells, and rear hubcap using the No. 12 chisel blender with Lamp Black (**Fig. 1**).

2. The front hubcap is more detailed with rust. Paint the rust spots using the No. 3 round with Dark Chocolate. While still wet, deepen with Lamp Black. Shade the hub using the No. 4 chisel blender with Navy Blue, then highlight with Snow White. Line the wheels with Lamp Black (**Fig. 2**).

3. Use the 1/8" lunar blender to apply the rust with Lamp Black, Turquoise Blue, Dark Chocolate, Traditional Burnt Sienna, and Burnt Orange (**Fig. 3**).

Lettering

Note: Refer to Tips & Techniques on page 10.

1. Use the liner with Desert Turquoise + Navy Blue (2:1) to letter "WEBSTER'S TOWING".

2. Use the short liner with Heritage Brick to letter "24 Hour Road Service".

Finish

1. Antique as described in Tips & Techniques on page 10.

2. When dry, spray with Sealer/Finisher. Let dry.

3. Place the insert into the tray.

Fig. 3

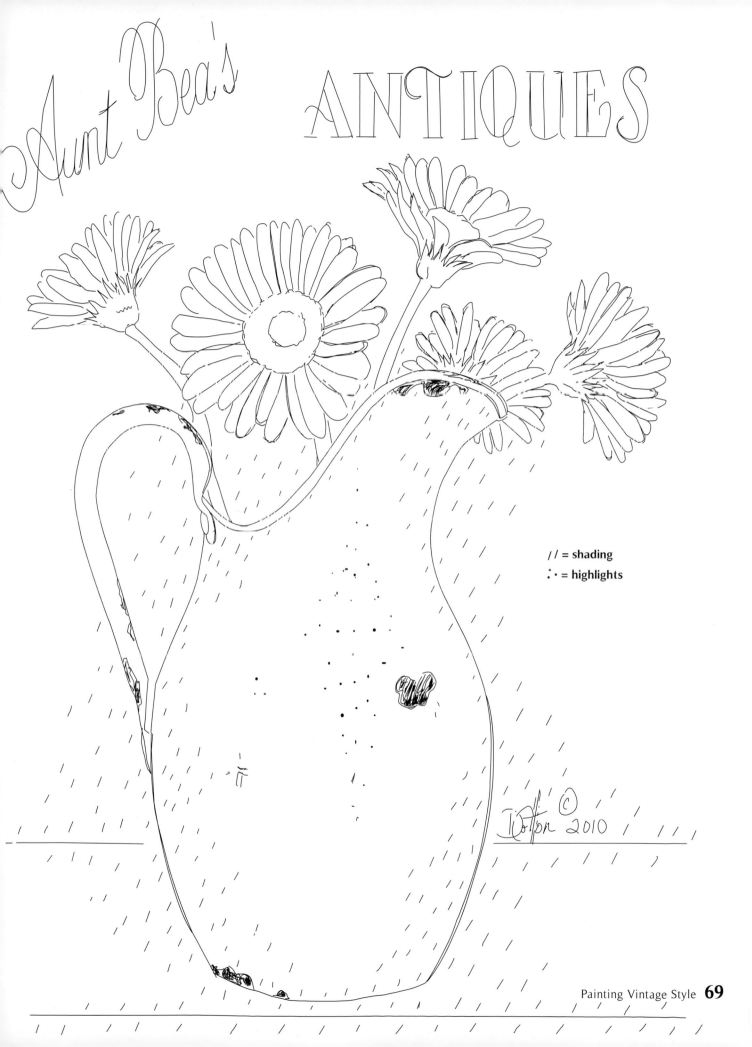

// = shading

∴• = highlights

// = shading

∴∙ = highlights

GREENFIELD CARRIAGE CO.

For All Of Your Hauling Needs!

RAISINS

FEEDS & NEEDS CO.

SUNNYSIDE

Dotti © 2011

Rooster

#2

#3

#1

#4

**Enlarge just
the rooster
pattern to 125%;
lettering pattern is
actual size.**

73

NEW YORK KENNEL CLUB

Breeding
Champions
Since 1898

**Enlarge
pattern to 125%**

PERKINS FRUIT WHOLESALERS

Hand Packed Since 1901

Freshness Guaranteed

// = shading
: = highlights

ALLEY CAT

LICORICE CO.

World's Finest

Ten For A Penny

/ / = shading
∴ = highlights

STONY CREEK BLACKSMITHS

// = shading

∴ = highlights

AUTOMOTIVE SERVICE & REPAIR

Clancy's

We Can Fix Anything!

Windy Ridge FARM

Dotton ©2011

**Enlarge
pattern to 125%**

// = shading
∴ = highlights

24 HOUR
ROAD
SERVICE

© 2011
JCotton

**Enlarge
pattern to 125%**

// = shading

∴ = highlights

NEW ENGLAND TIN WORKS

Est. 1860

Enlarge
pattern to 125%

Debbie Cotton

Debbie is known within the decorative painting industry for her signature vintage style, and she has been teaching and designing for the past sixteen years. Although Debbie began her career painting in oil, the primary medium she uses today is acrylic. Her teaching style is both relaxed and educational, and she offers a wealth of information for any level of painter. Debbie's ability to teach as well as she paints makes her a sought-after instructor, and she has traveled throughout North America to share her painting techniques with hundreds of students. You can find Debbie's designs, painting kits, letterings, stencils, and brushes on her website (www.simply-cotton.com). Contact her at simplycotton@xplornet.com.